Doing Business on the World-Wide Web

by
Marni C. Patterson

DOING BUSINESS ON THE WORLD-WIDE WEB

Marni C. Patterson

CREDITS
Managing Editor: *Kathleen Barcos*
Editor: *Kay Keppler*
Designer: *ExecuStaff*
Typesetting: *ExecuStaff*
Cover Design: *London Road Design*

All rights reserved. No part of this book may be reproduced or transmitted in any form or by any means now known or to be invented, electronic or mechanical, including photocopying, recording, or by any information storage or retrieval system without written permission from the author or publisher, except for the brief inclusion of quotations in a review.

Copyright © 1997 by Crisp Publications, Inc.

Printed in the United States of America by Bawden Printing Company.

Library of Congress Catalog Card Number 96-85520
Patterson, Marni
Doing Business on the World-Wide Web
ISBN 1-56052-390-5

# Preface

Unless you've been asleep for the past year or so, you can't help but have heard about the hottest phenomenon to hit the electronics and telecommunications industry since the desktop computer. It's the Internet, gateway to the information superhighway and the catalyst that is changing the way we communicate and do business. Many say the Internet is to the 1990s what television was to the 1950s. Some say that within 10 years, we'll spend more time "surfing the Net" than watching network TV.

To many, the Internet means the World-Wide Web or Web. As shown by its explosive growth over the past couple of years, thousands of companies have recognized the World-Wide Web as a valuable marketing and promotions tool. To compete in the future, the Web *must* be included as part of your marketing mix. This book will show you how to take advantage of this new medium to improve service to present customers and attract new ones.

About the Book

If you want to increase your business, provide better and faster service for your customers and reach prospective customers throughout the world, you need to consider marketing on the Web. Are you sold but the owner or boss isn't? Are you and the boss or owner sold but don't know where to start? If you answered yes to either of these questions, this book is for you.

About the Author

Marni Patterson is the owner of International Business Ventures Unlimited, which specializes in the establishment of joint ventures between U.S.-based high-technology companies and partners located in Europe and the Pacific Rim.

She received degrees in business, communications, and international relations from Syracuse University.

> Marni C. Patterson
> 9571 E. Caldwell Dr.
> Tucson, AZ 85747
> 520-574-9353
> 520-574-0620 (fax)
> cogent@indirect.com

Contents

Preface iii
Introduction xi

SECTION I   STARTING UP 1
    Equipment You'll Need 3
    On-line Service or ISP 4

SECTION II   LET'S GET CONNECTED 7
    Locating Web Sites 9
    Navigating the Web 10

SECTION III   A WEB PAGE OF YOUR OWN 17
    Design Tips 20
    Should I Do It Myself or Hire Someone? 24
    Case Study—Soundview Executive Book Summaries 26
    Case Study—Presence Information Design 27

The Design and Planning Process 28
Examples of Effective Web Sites 30

SECTION IV   PLANNING AND ORGANIZING A WEB PAGE 39

Subject Company 41
Elements to Include 42
Case Analysis 44

SECTION V   GETTING NOTICED 47

Server Strategy 49
Search Engines 53
Newsgroups 54
Linking with Other Web Pages 56
On-line Advertising 57
Support Your Web Site in Other Advertising 57
Cybermalls 57

SECTION VI   MEASURING SUCCESS 61

Getting a Reaction 63
Tools and Resources 65

SECTION VII WEB-BASED BUSINESS IDEAS 71
    Direct Sales 74
    Selling Ad Space 76
    Selling Subscriptions 77
    On-line Services 77

SECTION VIII THWARTING HACKERS AND CYPHERPUNKS 81
    Concerning Security Issues 83
    Resources and Tools 85
    Does All This Really Work? 88

SECTION IX THE FUTURE OF THE WEB 91
    Hot Java 93
    Three-Dimensional Web Sites 93
    Common Client Interface 95
    The Many Languages of the Web 95

In Conclusion 102
Resource Directory 103
Glossary 111
References 121

Acknowledgments

I'd like to thank the following people for their help on this book.

Alex Dely, Tucson Transatlantic Trade and Chapman College, for providing access to trade publications and other information sources.

Jeff Olson, Soundview Executive Book Summaries (Middlebury, VT), and Brad King; Presence Information Design (Pasadena, CA), for their insight about what separates a good Web Site from a great one.

The many people who shared their experiences and anecdotes about how the Internet and World-Wide Web helped their companies.

Dedication

This book is dedicated to James G. (Jim) Patterson, my husband and author of two books for Crisp Publications. He was the world's best sounding board while I was writing, and his technical expertise with computers, on-line services and the Internet was appreciated during editing and proofing.

Introduction

We are in the midst of a cyberspace revolution. Desktop computers and fax machines began the wave during the 1980s, and many predict the Internet and World-Wide Web will continue it in the 1990s.

For the past couple of years, it's been virtually impossible to read any newspaper or magazine without seeing an article about the Internet or the Information Superhighway. Most businesspeople now have an e-mail address in addition to phone and fax numbers.

As most cyberfanatics will tell you, however, the real news lately has been the growth of the World-Wide Web, or simply, the Web. With its endless library of graphic-intensive, interactive sites or "pages" stored on computer servers throughout the world, the Web has made it possible to do things with computers we never would have dreamed possible, even a few years ago. Web surfers can take a college course, open a bank account, buy or sell stock, make an airline or hotel reservation or preview a new movie, all without leaving their computer screens.

The Web is the fastest-growing area of the Internet. During 1994, statistics showed that three to four million users were surfing the Web. In 1995, the Web doubled in size every four to six months, largely because America Online, Prodigy, and CompuServe, the three largest on-line services, began offering their users Web access. Microsoft Corporation added another 1.3 million potential users with its Internet Explorer web browser which is included with every copy of Windows 95. Not wanting to be left out of the cyber rush, AT&T and MCI are both offering Internet access to their present customers, and use attractive pricing for Internet access as a marketing tool to attract new customers.

Growth of Web Traffic

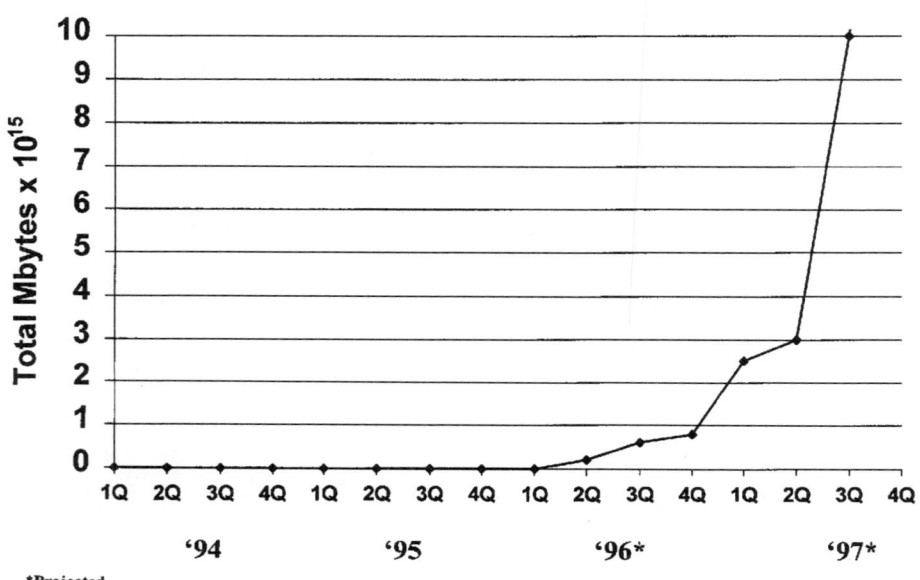

*Projected
Source: The Internet Society

These users have a lot to check out. Lycos, Inc., Marlboro, MA, a company that catalogs the Web on a daily basis, estimated that in early 1996 there were about 19 million web sites. If the Web doubled in size every four months and growth were to continue at this rate, there would be about 150 million web pages by the end of 1996.

According to a study by O'Reilly & Associates, a leading publisher of books about on-line communications in Sebastopol, CA, 5.8 million adults now have Internet access at work or home, and an additional 3.9 million use commercial on-line services only. The study predicts that the on-line community will grow by six million adults during the next year. Some experts predict there will be 50 million users by 1996, close to 100 million by 1998, and a whopping 200 million users by the year 2000.

Companies have gotten the message that the Web is the advertising medium of the future. Commercial users lead the way in the explosion in demand for web sites. The number of commercial web pages increased by more than *three million* in less than a year.

According to ActivMedia, Inc., an authority on on-line market analysis, research and market trends located in Petersbourgh, NH, the number of businesses advertising their products and services on-line grows by about 34% each month. That rate is expected to increase, since "user friendly" software and shareware programs are making it easier for anyone to design a professional-looking web site.

Not to be outdone, companies that sell word processing and desktop publishing software are also getting into the act. Future upgrades of Adobe Pagemaker will include the ability to convert text, pictures and graphics into web sites, and other companies are expected to follow suit by revising their products.

The Internet and World-Wide Web will have a profound effect on the way businesses market their products, because both the Internet and Web intersect with, and in some cases supersede, traditional broadcasting and publishing media. You can find shifts toward electronic commerce in every sector of our society.

Newspapers have seen their mechanical and labor costs rise with big increases in newsprint and postage and revenues fall because of the advent of niche publications and loss of market share to television and radio. To combat this trend, some papers are going on-line. The *San Jose Mercury News*, for example, charges a fee for on-line readers to see completely new material. The *New York Times* makes its archive available for downloading, charging for each article accessed. Direct marketing companies face higher printing costs and postal rates, making the prospect of selling on the Web even more attractive for businesses. Home banking on-line will become the norm, much as ATM machines became the norm about 15 years ago. Local governments have web pages, and some analysts predict that before too long, voting on-line will be possible. One microbrewery even sold its stock on-line.

This move toward cyberspace communications as the basis for business-to-business transactions and as the main interaction and information channel for consumer markets is happening now. Organizations that recognize the challenges and potential of this change will prosper in the future. So, get ready!

SECTION ONE

Starting Up

The Web was developed at CERN, a Swiss research lab, in 1989 as a tool to link physicists worldwide. It didn't gain much in popularity outside scientific circles until about 1993, when the availability of faster computers and modems that could handle the Web's graphic interface made it more appealing to individual and commercial users. The introduction of Mosaic, the first web browsing software that could read the hypertext markup language (HTML) with which web pages are written, also was crucial.

Equipment You'll Need

Because the Web is graphic intensive, a 486 computer or the equivalent is a must. You also need a mouse, graphical user interface (GUI) program such as Windows, Macintosh or OS/2, and a modem, preferably 14,400 bauds per second (bps) or faster. As most veteran World-Wide Web users will tell you, "surfing" the Web at 9,600 bps or less is excruciatingly slow unless you use the "text only" feature. But why miss out on the Web's main attraction—the graphics, sound and animation capabilities?

To access the Internet, either subscribe to one of the on-line services or contract Internet service with an Internet Service Provider (ISP). All the larger on-line services such as Prodigy, America Online and CompuServe offer connections to the Internet. If you have Windows 95, you have access to Microsoft's Internet Explorer. If you would rather use an ISP, look in the business section of your local newspaper or in any computer or Internet magazine for companies' ads.

Web pages are typically designed with text and graphics, photographs, video animation, digitized sound files or a combination of these. This material is written and designed using HTML (hypertext markup language), and you'll need a web browser to decipher it so you can read it.

Starting Up

4

All web browsers are based on one of three systems—Netscape's Navigator, Mosaic or Microsoft's Internet Explorer. At this writing, Netscape has the largest share of the market with Internet Explorer gaining; Mosaic is in third place and losing ground. For information about specific browsers, check computer industry magazines (*MacUser, PC World, PC Computing,* etc.) for product reviews. Some companies offer a 30-day free trial period or a "demo" you can download from the Web. Clarify what type of computer or software is required with each browser so that you choose something compatible with your system. You'll find a list of web browsers in the Resource Directory at the end of this book.

Some other items you might find useful include a sound card, speakers and an accelerated graphics card. These aren't absolutely necessary, but they will make your web surfing much more enjoyable.

On-line Service or ISP

Should you subscribe to an on-line service for access to the Internet rather than use an ISP? It depends. Subscribing to an on-line service is usually more expensive. However, you may also have access to libraries, free software, travel and other services that you probably won't have through an ISP.

One disadvantage of subscribing to an on-line services: you may be locked into using the e-mail, news reader and web browser program of that service whether you like it or not. You're free to use the programs of your choice with an ISP. However, all three of the major on-line services have recently become more flexible about this.

One of the things you're paying for if you subscribe to an on-line service is access to free software—including web browsers—a perk that most ISPs don't provide. All three of the major on-line services provide web browsers for their subscribers. For Prodigy, access requires just one

Doing Business on the World-Wide Web

mouse click from Prodigy's main screen to download the software. Then Prodigy updates the software each time you jump to Prodigy's web section.

CompuServe offers web access outside its WinCIM and MacCIM software using any commercial web browser program. You can also use Netlauncher (Go Netlauncher) or Point-to-Point Protocol (PPP) Internet Access (Go PPP).

America Online offers web access for Windows users as part of its regular service through a web browser program called Internet Works. For Mac users, America Online has licensed the use of Connect II, a web browser program developed by Intercom Systems Corp.

Starting Up

6

Section I Review

1. Where was the Web invented and why?

2. Name two ways you can access the Web.

3. What language is used to write web pages?

4. Do you have a web browser program? If so, which one? If you answered no, answer question 4a.

4a. *(Skip this question if you have a web browser program.)* Read about the web browsers available on the market. Then, visit your local computer store and choose one.

5. Complete the following checklist to make sure you have all the equipment and resources needed to surf the Web.

   - ❏ 486 computer (or equivalent)
   - ❏ Mouse
   - ❏ Graphical User Interface
   - ❏ Sound Card (optional)
   - ❏ Accelerated graphics card (optional)
   - ❏ Modem (14,400 bps or higher)
   - ❏ Web browser program
   - ❏ Access to the Internet
   - ❏ Speakers (optional)

Doing Business on the World-Wide Web

S E C T I O N T W O

Let's Get Connected

Picture a huge library where you can find information on any subject, where all the books have color pictures and graphics, and where some even have narration or animation abilities. Your card catalog is called a search engine, and you locate information by using one or two key words. (You can also find a specific web site by using its "call number" or Uniform Resource Locator (URL), which is its address on the Web.)

Locating Web Sites

Some of the more commonly used search engines on the Web are called Yahoo!, Excite, Altavista and Lycos. The more traditional search engines usually associated with text-only files on the Internet (i.e., Archie, Veronica and Gopher) are also accessible through the Web. All these require is a key word or group of words to search for information.

You can find any web page as long as you have the *exact* web page address, or URL, by using the "Open" command under the File menu. All URLs are formatted as follows: *HTTP://gnn.com/gnn.html*. The HTTP stands for Hyper Text Transport Protocol, and the slashes are forward slashes—not backwards the way users familiar with DOS are accustomed to seeing. In the example, *gnn.com* refers to the server on which the information is located and *gnn.html* refers to the file name and the format in which it's written. So in "Web lingo," what you'd be asking your web browser to do if you requested it to draw this URL is *"use the Hyper Text Transport Protocol to find the file named gnn, which is written in Hypertext Markup Language, and is located on the gnn.com server."*

Many companies that have web pages list their URL in other advertising. If you copy one of these addresses to access it later, be sure you copy it *exactly* as shown. Likewise, when you put your URL in your own print or radio/TV advertising, check to make sure the URL is correct.

Let's Get Connected

Once you find the web site you're looking for using either of these methods, you can see it on your monitor complete with color photos, graphics and sometimes sound and animation. You can also pick and choose the information you want by clicking with your mouse on hyperlinks, or key words, which lead to additional information and sometimes to another web site altogether.

Navigating the Web

These procedures will all make much more sense once you see them in action. Therefore the remainder of this chapter will be interactive, and will refer to the illustration below. This is the start page (opening screen view) you see when you sign on to the Web using Microsoft Corporation's Internet Explorer 3.0. If you're using a browser other than Internet Explorer 3.0, the appearance of the start page and terminology used will differ from what you see in the following illustration.

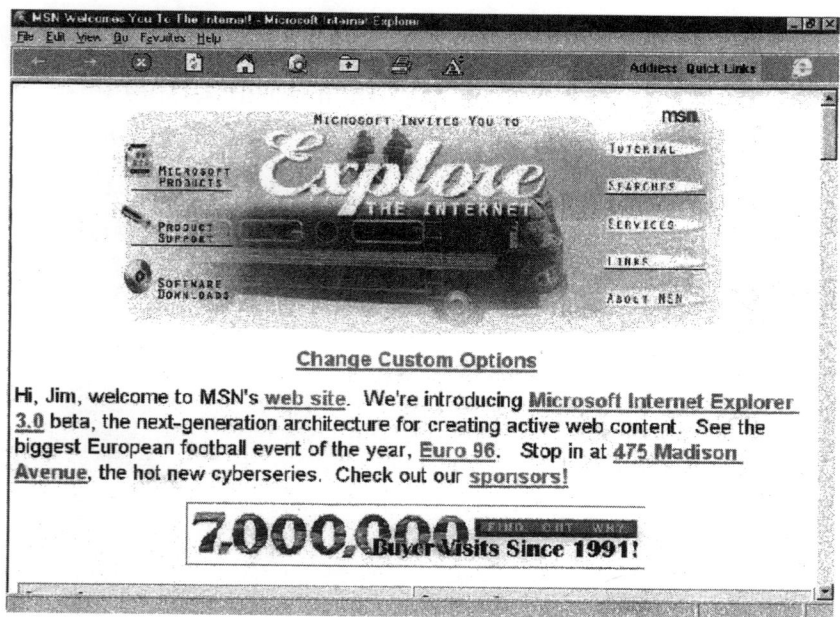

Doing Business on the World-Wide Web

11

> Sign on to the Web and let's go surfing!

If you're accustomed to using a mouse and are familiar with the pull-down menus used in Mac- and Windows-based programs, what you see will look familiar. In addition to the pull-down menus, you have a toolbar with buttons which make it easier to navigate your way around a web page. Here's a list of commands you'll use most frequently along with a description of where you can find them.

- **Search** (located on pull-down menu under "Go" and on tool bar as a globe with a magnifying glass)—Provides list of search engines (e.g., Lycos, Altavista, etc.).

- **Favorites** (located on pull-down menu and on tool bar as a folder with an asterisk)—Enables you to keep a list of web pages you'd like to access frequently. Called "Bookmark" for Netscape browser users.

- **Back** (Located on pull-down menu under "Go" and on tool bar as a left arrow)—Takes you back within a web site to the screen you just left.

- **Forward** (Located on pull-down menu under "Go" and on tool bar as a right arrow)—Takes you forward within a web site to the screen you were just viewing.

- **Home** (Located on tool bar as a house)—Exits out of whatever web page you're in and takes you back to the start or home page.

- **Reload** (Located on pull-down menu under "View" and on tool bar as a page with two curved arrows)—Reloads the web site you're currently viewing or have just finished viewing.

- **Stop** (Located on pull-down menu under "View" and on tool bar as a red circle with a white "X")—Stops your browser from draw-

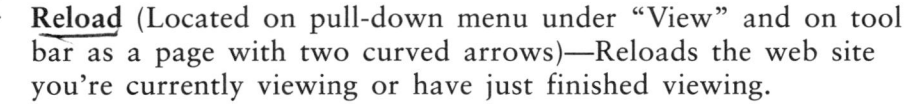

Let's Get Connected

ing a web site (or component thereof) so you can move on to something else.

> **Take a minute to find each of the commands on your screen.**

To see how all these features work together, let's first access a web site using one of the search engines. You have a choice of many search engines which will help you find information on virtually any subject when you supply one or two key words.

> **Click on "Go" and then "Search" the Internet, or click on the picture of the globe with the magnifying glass.**

The next screen you see will offer you a choice of five search engines depending on which ones you specified when you installed your web browser. In Internet Explorer 3.0, these include: Excite, Infoseek, Lycos, Yahoo!, and Magellan.

> **Choose one of the search engines and move the cursor to the rectangular box beside it. Click your mouse once so that the cursor appears in the box next to the search engine of your choice. Type in a subject word of your choice, and then click on the box that says "Search."**

Doing Business on the World-Wide Web

If the search engine can't find anything on that subject or word, it will tell you. If this happens, choose another subject and try again. If it finds web pages which address the subject of your search, it will list them so you can review the list.

> **Choose one of the web sites which sounds interesting to you and click on it with your mouse.**

While you wait for the web page you've chosen to appear on your monitor, look at the top right-hand corner of your screen. You'll see a lower-case "e" with a circle around it flashing. Sometimes you'll also see a blue dotted line in the bottom right-hand corner expanding in size from left to right. Both these actions signify that your browser is accessing the components of the web site you've requested from the server, or servers, where they're located.

You should now be on the first page, or home page, of the web site you've chosen. In all likelihood, you're looking at general company or organizational information and maybe some graphics and a photo or two. As you maneuver around the home page with your mouse, you'll notice certain words are shown in a contrasting color. These are called hyperlinks, and clicking on them with your mouse will enable you to access more information within this web site, or even connect to other web sites.

> **Choose a hyperlink of your choice and click on it with your mouse.**

Let's Get Connected

14

Remember, if you don't like what you see once you get there, you can always use the "Backward" command to take you back to the previous page. On most well-designed web pages, there's also a hyperlink at the bottom of each page which will take you back to the home page.

> **Choose another hyperlink and practice maneuvering throughout this same web site. Then return to the home page.**

On the home page of many web sites, there's a hyperlink which will enable you to send an e-mail message to the company or organization.

> **Find the e-mail feature if there is one on the site you've chosen and click on it with your mouse. If you want to send a message, do it now in the space provided. Otherwise, just look at how the e-mail section of the web page is designed.**

When you're finished, go back to the home page. Go to the top of your screen again and click on "Home." This will take you back to your opening screen once more. Congratulations! You've just successfully navigated your first web page.

Doing Business on the World-Wide Web

Section II Review

1. Sign on to the Web and choose a search engine other than the one you used during the interactive session. Conduct a search on another subject. Access one of the web sites that appears on the list and cruise around. Repeat using different search engines until you feel comfortable using search engines and navigating your way around web pages.

2. Find three web site addresses in your local newspaper (look in ads and at the end of news articles) or in one of your favorite magazines. Sign on to the Web and open each web site using the open command under "File."

SECTION THREE

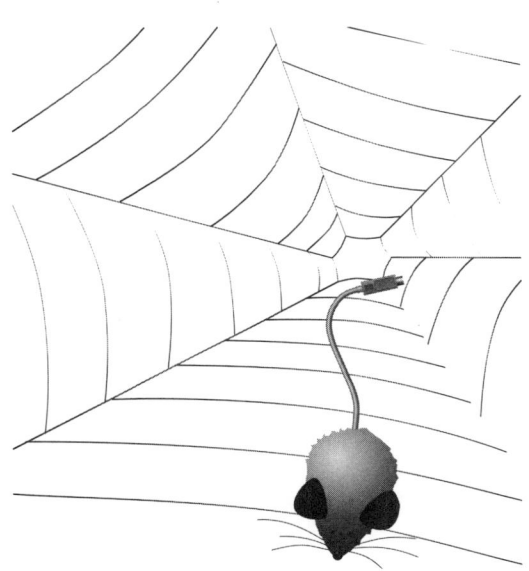

A Web Page of Your Own

 *You've heard the rumors and the hype. You've heard that "everybody who's anybody" is on the World-Wide Web—but you're still wondering: What are the advantages for me? Each company is different, but most would agree that the following reasons summarize the advantages of having a web page.*

Thirteen Reasons

- ♦ You control the process from beginning to end without having to rely on printers, media buyers or anyone else. (This also means you don't have to pay expensive advertising agency rates for these services.)

- ♦ It's inexpensive. With many products, you can reduce your marketing and distribution costs significantly, as well as provide service after the sale at very little cost to you and your customers.

- ♦ It's easy to establish one-on-one communication directly with customers since they come to you for information.

- ♦ You receive immediate feedback on your marketing campaign from potential customers. This means you can make any changes and adjustments needed immediately—and again, inexpensively.

- ♦ Your marketing message can be tailored to meet the specific needs of each customer and delivered immediately by e-mail.

- ♦ You can reduce overhead costs by receiving and processing orders using the Web.

- ♦ If you're a small business, you can finally compete with big corporations on a level playing field. The Web is the great equalizer when it comes to company size.

A Web Page of Your Own

- You can market your products and services around the world at no extra cost.

- It's easy to measure the effectiveness of your web page, since you know how many hits and visits you receive per day.

- You can also track the effectiveness of your web site by offering a special available only to customers who order on-line.

- There's no delay between customers seeing your page and placing an order immediately, an advantage that print and TV ads can't provide.

- The hypermedia capabilities of the Web enable you to show pictures and photographs of products and offer animated and narrated product demonstrations, all without incurring costs for personal sales calls and postage for mailing information.

- You can make your web site as interactive as you'd like to encourage longer visits from users and potential customers. Ultimately, customers become more familiar with your company and products, making it more likely that they will place orders sooner.

Design Tips

"OK, I'm sold," you say, "I want to develop my own web page, but where do I begin?" Let's start with some basics of designing web sites so you'll understand the elements of a well-designed web page.

Plan Ahead. Your mother and your fifth grade teacher were right—it really does pay to plan ahead. Figure out what you want your web site to accomplish and map out your site on paper first. This way, you can see if ideas and pages flow the way you want them to, and if users can access information in a logical order. Then execute your paper plan on the computer and test it on-line to make doubly sure everything works in an orderly fashion. Make any changes and adjustments needed. When you're finished and are certain everything's just the way you want it, test it again just to be sure.

Use the KISS Principle (Keep It Short and Simple). Don't overload your web site with too much information. Users have a shorter attention span when reading a computer screen than a reader has with a newspaper, magazine or book. The most important thing to remember is, think simply and logically. Don't neglect graphics and photos, but concentrate on presenting your ideas in a clear, easy-to-follow fashion.

Choose Colors that Contrast. Make it as easy as possible for users to read the contents of your web site. Be sure the background color you choose is light or dark enough to offset the color you choose for the text. Choose a color for your hyperlink words that contrasts with both the background and regular text colors.

Keep Your Style Consistent. Visitors to your web page will become accustomed to reading information in a similar format in each section, and seeing the same colors and similar type styles. Although it may be tempting to use the entire color spectrum and every innovative font in your typeface repertoire, you'll only confuse site visitors if you do. Choose a color scheme you like and stay with it throughout your entire web site. Set comprehensive style guides before you begin and stick to them. Headlines should always be the same typeface and size. If you decide to use asterisks before each item in a list, don't switch to dots or diamonds in another section. If you decide to highlight one section title, they should all be highlighted.

Check for Language Barriers. Are you targeting your web site to people who may feel more comfortable using another language? An easy solution is to post your home page in the language most of your audience uses, and then give customers an option to see additional material in other languages. Contract with a professional translator to write the foreign language sections. You may think you learned enough French or Spanish back in high school to do this yourself, but veterans of international marketing agree: When accuracy matters, pay a professional translator. You'll be glad you did.

A Web Page of Your Own

Easy Does It with the Graphics and Photos. The Web is so impressive that your first inclination will be to include your largest, most impressive product photos and graphics. Don't! Graphics and photos take longer to draw when users are trying to view your web page, and many users, especially those with slower modems, move on to some other page if the one they're trying to draw is too slow to appear. Limit each graphic or photo to no more than 40,000–50,000 bytes, which keeps them large enough to see and read easily, but small enough to download quickly.

If you can't resist including a photo or graphic that requires a lot of draw time, place it somewhere so that the user can still get access to other information on your web site without drawing it. In other words, don't put it on your home page so that everyone who visits your web page must wait for the download. You can also have your web site draw the photo or graphic at 40,000 to 50,000 bytes and offer users the option of increasing the size using a separate link.

Reuse graphics whenever possible (such as company logo, address and telephone number, product photos, etc.). Once a browser has drawn a photo or graphic image once, it can show that same photo or graphic again and again during the same visit without using additional time to draw it.

Although it's tempting to add all sorts of pretty pictures and fancy graphics that demand a great deal of draw time, remember that your web site is useless if potential customers never see it because they get frustrated trying to access it.

Offer a Text-Only Option. Here's another solution if you want to use complex graphics without inconveniencing users who have slower modems. Offer users the option to switch to a text-only mode. For two good examples on how this looks to the user, see Sun Microsystem's web site at *http://www.sun.com*, and Digital Equipment Corporation's web site at *http://www.digital.com*. When you're finished designing your web page, do a test run in both modes to make sure everything makes sense and looks appealing.

Doing Business on the World-Wide Web

Steal Code (or Just Borrow It). If you see a page design or layout, type style, or graphics placement in another web page that you like, copy the code and use it. However, if you see a photo, graphic or drawing that you'd like to copy and use, contact the company or web page designer first and ask permission. Most are very happy to oblige, unless what you want to use is proprietary or restricted in some way. Do not under any circumstances scan album or CD covers, pictures or cartoons from magazines, newspapers and books, or company symbols and logos unless you obtain written permission from the company or the publisher. These images are protected by copyright law, and you could be fined or sued if you were held in violation.

Make it Easy to Order On-line. Be sure to incorporate a "shopping cart" feature in your web site to make it convenient for visitors to order from you. You can easily do this by placing a button which says "Select" or "Put in Shopping Cart" next to each item in your on-line catalog. To order an item, all the visitor needs to do is click the box next to the item, and the item is automatically placed on the order form. It's also a good idea to include a button on each page that says "View Contents of Shopping Cart," or "View Order Form" so customers can check what they've ordered so far.

Empower Potential Customers. A web site offers you two opportunities to communicate with your customers that no print or television ad can match. First, the design of a web page enables visitors to choose the infor-mation they want to see about you and your company. This creates an opportunity for you to package your products' features and benefits so customers receive the information you want to emphasize. Secondly, the interactive nature of the Web allows you to use it as a sales tool as well as a marketing tool by offering your customers the immediate opportunity to ask questions, request information, give you feedback, compare prices or place an order—all without leaving their computers.

Watch Out for Dead Ends. In the rush to be on the Web, many companies have made their web sites available even though they're not quite finished. For the areas where the information isn't yet available, the page

A Web Page of Your Own

says "Under Construction" or "Unfinished." You'll score a lot of points with potential customers if you indicate on your home page which parts of your web site are still under construction so they don't waste time accessing pages that have no information. Nothing frustrates visitors to your web page more than to work through all kinds of links to get to something that sounds interesting only to see "under construction" or "unfinished' on the page. If a page or section isn't ready, say so on page one, list it as a "soon-to-be offered" feature or service or don't list it at all until it's ready.

Above all, when you're designing your web page, remember that you're working with an entirely different medium with new guidelines and requirements. Simply reproducing your latest magazine ad or the company brochure on the Web is not the solution. This is the same mistake many companies made when television first appeared. They found out very quickly that their successful radio ads were total flops when transferred to television.

Should I Do It Myself or Hire Someone?

Creating your own web page doesn't need to be a frustrating or intimidating experience. Many web page design software programs are available through on-line services, shareware and commercially that make it easy for anyone to design professional-looking web pages.

Some programs require a good working knowledge of HTML coding, but many of the newer programs enable you to design a nice-looking web site with little (if any) knowledge of HTML. However, for more elaborate page layouts and fancy graphics and features, you'll still need to acquire some understanding of HTML. For a good example of a self-contained program to put your company on-line, take a look at Web Series by SBT Internet Systems (San Rafael, CA). Web Series is a three-module program which enables you to: design your own web site, process orders and control stock and inventory, track and measure your web page traffic, and even rent

Doing Business on the World-Wide Web

server space. For more information, access SBT Internet Systems's web site at *http://www.sbt.com.*

Check computer magazines for product reviews and recommendations. There's also a list of some of the web page designer programs in the Resource Directory at the end of this book. The larger on-line services provide simple web design software for their members. If you subscribe to one of the on-line services instead of an ISP, be sure to check out this option.

If you have neither the time nor the inclination to design your own web page, there are companies springing up all over that specialize in designing and maintaining web pages on a contractual basis. If you choose to contract with a company to design and maintain your web site, most veterans of the process will attest that it pays to shop around.

This industry is new and growing fast, and prices and levels of service vary a great deal. Check prices carefully and find out exactly what work and services are included in the quoted price. Look at examples of the designer's work.

To find designers whose work you like, surf the Web, paying close attention to design and use of color, as well as correct spelling and grammar. Check the credits (usually at the bottom of the home page), and you'll know whom to contact for a quote.

Each company uses its own set of criteria to estimate labor and time needed for each web page. Where one vendor might offer nice, turn-key results for $400, another company might charge $800 or even $1,200 for the same thing.

Don't forget to figure in maintenance costs for the designer to change and update the information on your web site. It will be ineffective if you just build it and walk away. You should expect to update information at least once weekly.

A Web Page of Your Own

If you aren't having any satisfaction finding a designer you like at a price you can afford by surfing the Web and choosing web sites you like, visit three web pages that list design firms: *http://search.yahoo.com/bin/search?p=Web+Page+Design*, *http://www.elc.gnn.com/bus/index.html*, and *http://www.activmedia.com*. The Activmedia web site has a form you complete where YOU specify what you want in a web page designer (i.e., price range, services required, etc.), and the web site refers your request to those firms listed so they can contact you and offer a quote.

Case Study—Soundview Executive Book Summaries

No one but you can decide whether designing your own page or having it done by someone else will work best for you. If you're thinking about doing the work yourself, consider the experience of Soundview Executive Book Summaries (Middlebury, VT). Soundview publishes and distributes summaries of books of interest to managerial- and executive-level employees at all types and sizes of companies. It also stocks and sells complete copies of the books it summarizes in cooperation with other publishers. Its subscribers in the United States and Canada and in more than 129 other countries value these summaries as a screening mechanism to decide whether they wish to read or buy an entire book and because they find the summaries useful as a reference tool.

According to Jeff Olson, Soundview editor and creator of the company's web site, Soundview decided to do the web page design and writing work in-house because many software programs enable companies to create their own web page, and because there was so much variance in quotes for the work and site maintenance with no real guarantee of quality or results. Soundview also needed to decide whether to invest in a telephone line dedicated for Internet use, or to lease space in one of the cybermalls located on the Web. If neither of these, then what?

Doing Business on the World-Wide Web

Soundview solved the dilemma by affiliating with a catalog web site where the company that owns the site provides the computer server and T1 line, but lessees are responsible for the design and maintenance of their own web page.

How has it worked? "Great," says Olson, who adds that Soundview has no regrets and would still elect to do the design and maintenance work in-house if they had to do it over again. As for results, after only nine months on the Web, Soundview's web site generated "more new subscriptions that we ever would have expected" along with book orders. Olson points out that Soundview's web page is linked to its publishers' web pages, and that many of them also have received hits as a result of Soundview's web site. For further information about Soundview's experiences designing and maintaining a web page in-house visit Soundview's web site at *http://www.summary.com* or contact Jeff Olson at *jolson@interserv.com*.

Case Study—Presence Information Design

If designing and maintaining your web site is something you'd rather leave to the pros, consider the results Presence Information Design (Pasadena, CA) has obtained for its clients. Presence Information Design has designed and maintained web pages for companies such as Hot, Hot, Hot!, a company that distributes hot sauces, Columbia Pictures, and Earthcycle, a national recycling program. The company is negotiating to design and maintain web pages for a specialty retail chain that plans to expand nationally and for a mail order firm.

Presence Information Design designs, maintains and provides a server for clients' web sites. It also includes the marketing of new web pages once they are on the Web by promoting and publicizing them through newsgroups and search engines. It has also designed a mechanism that is incorporated into each web page it designs, which helps track the number of hits to all web sites and monitor resulting sales.

A Web Page of Your Own

According to Brad King, sales vice president, companies contract with Presence Information Design because they don't have the time to learn the intricacies of HTML or update the web site as often as needed and "want a unique web page that will attract attention."

Many of Presence Information Design's clients have gotten their wish. One of Presence's web sites was awarded the Champion of Cyberspace award at the first National Information Infrastructure competition, and another web site won an award for best business Internet site in that competition.

Hot, Hot, Hot! has received national publicity and is ranked in the top five percent of the best revenue-generating sites on the Web. American Gramophone, the distribution and recording company for Mannheim Steamroller, recorded thousands of hits and many orders per month in the first 10 months of its web site operation.

For further information about Presence Information Design's services and experiences designing and maintaining web pages, visit Presence's web site at *http://www.presence.com* or contact Brad King at *bradk@presence.com*.

The Design and Planning Process

Before you try to do anything on the computer, write down everything you'd like prospective customers to know about your company. Include information such as the products and services you offer, features and benefits of each, pictures or photographs of each, customer service and general information about your company.

Now divide everything into general categories such as company information, product divisions, individual product information, pricing, how to order and so forth.

Each of these areas will serve as a main category area and will appear on your home page as a link to further information in that category. To

Doing Business on the World-Wide Web

avoid having too much information on any one page, continue breaking down the information and providing more links to lead the customer to additional information on the same subject. It's easiest if you visualize this entire process as a large triangle where you begin at the top and work your way down as shown on the chart below.

Remember to include two links at the end of each page, one that will enable customers to go to the top of the present page, and the other to take them back to your home page. It's also a good idea to include two additional links on your home page, the first so customers can send you an e-mail message to ask questions or request additional information, and the second to link users to a guest book where you can ask (but not demand) that they complete a registration form or short questionnaire.

You'll also need an order form and links which give users the option to be on your mailing list to receive catalogs, newsletters and new product announcements. This is a great, inexpensive way to build a mailing list of potential customers who you know are interested in your product since *they* came to *you*. Other possible items to include in your web site, if possible and appropriate, are sound, animation, a product demonstration video or a newsletter.

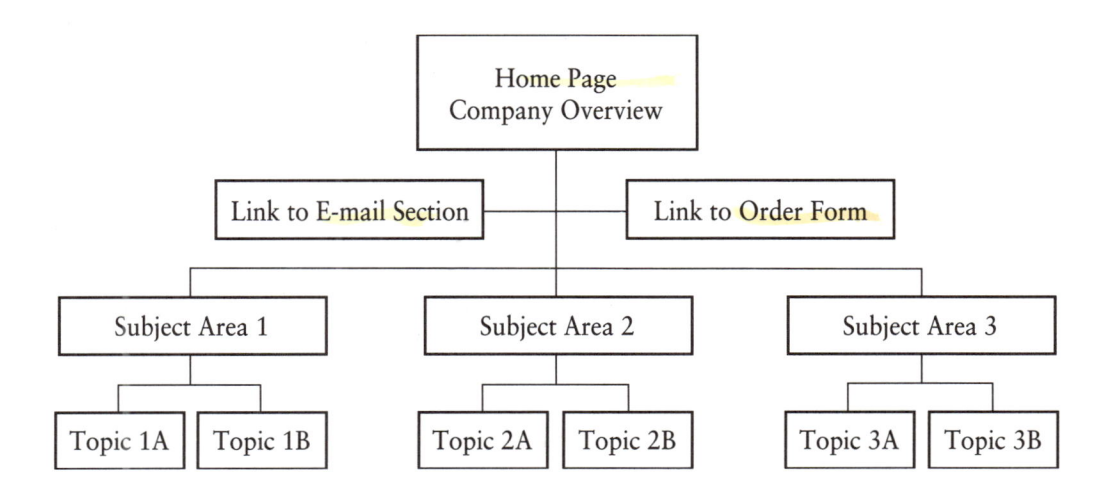

```
                    ┌─────────────────┐
                    │   Home Page     │
                    │ Company Overview│
                    └────────┬────────┘
              ┌──────────────┴──────────────┐
    ┌─────────────────────┐        ┌─────────────────────┐
    │ Link to E-mail Section │     │  Link to Order Form │
    └─────────────────────┘        └─────────────────────┘
         ┌──────────────────────┼──────────────────────┐
    ┌─────────────┐      ┌─────────────┐      ┌─────────────┐
    │ Subject Area 1 │   │ Subject Area 2 │   │ Subject Area 3 │
    └─────────────┘      └─────────────┘      └─────────────┘
      ┌─────┴─────┐        ┌─────┴─────┐        ┌─────┴─────┐
  ┌────────┐ ┌────────┐ ┌────────┐ ┌────────┐ ┌────────┐ ┌────────┐
  │Topic 1A│ │Topic 1B│ │Topic 2A│ │Topic 2B│ │Topic 3A│ │Topic 3B│
  └────────┘ └────────┘ └────────┘ └────────┘ └────────┘ └────────┘
```

A Web Page of Your Own

Examples of Effective Web sites

To see all these elements at work together, let's look at some existing web pages where the companies have done an excellent job of planning and organizing while integrating one or more design elements. These are web pages that impressed me. However, this doesn't mean they're the only well-designed web pages out there. Please view these as good examples, but find your own favorites as you cruise the Web.

Harley Davidson of Stamford, CT— (http://www.hd-stamford.com)

Harley-Davidson of Stamford, CT (HD) offers a lot of interesting information for easy and "not so easy" riders alike in a well-organized fashion. In addition to general company information, visitors have access to an on-line parts catalog, an on-line catalog for accessories and collectibles, information about new products and services, and a calendar of HD events in their area. Do you want to see your favorite Harley in action complete with sound effects? Download a video clip, or just click on one of the links on the home page for the sound only. Customers are encouraged to enter on-line contests to win HD clothing and collectibles, and to submit their own videos of themselves and their "hogs" with the incentive that they too could be a star if Harley-Davidson decides to include their video when they next update this web page.

Holiday Inn—(http://www.holiday-inn.com)

Whether their travels will include a stop in San Francisco or a week in Singapore, Holiday Inn offers visitors the ability to check room availability and rates, and make reservations, all without leaving the computer. An interactive map enables you to check prospective destinations for Holiday Inn locations. You can also request to see a picture of a particular Holiday Inn that interests you, a picture of a typical room, and a list of features at that particular location. Other web site links talk about current promotional programs and specials, and even give you the opportunity to contact the Chairman of the Board at Holiday Inn's Atlanta-based corporate headquarters. If you're really looking for the VIP treatment, interactive video tours are available of a few locations.

Intersport Great Britain, Ltd.— (http://www2.intersport.co.uk)

If you've ever watched a prominent sporting event and remember seeing the name Intersport advertised, you probably wondered what it was. Here's where you go to find out. Intersport is a worldwide association of retail sports equipment dealers who pool resources and purchasing power. There are currently about 3900 members of which 300 are located in the UK and Ireland. Visitors can find member stores in their respective areas by entering the name of a town or city, or by using an on-line map. There's also a link to enter the latest contest to win (what else?) various types of sporting goods. If you want to contact someone at Intersport or apply for membership, both are possible on-line.

Ragu Pizza Sauce "Mama's Cucina"— (http://www.eat.com)

If you're looking for a web site which is a good example of effective "soft" selling, this is the one! Visitors to "Mama's kitchen" are invited to list their favorite restaurants, submit dinner table stories, favorite recipes, and to complete a detailed (!) questionnaire which asks for opinions and habits on shopping, eating and buying habits. And believe it or not, people take the time to complete the entire thing, proving that interactive web pages really do work. There's a link where you can learn various Italian phrases, and another where you get a travelogue of Italy, complete with accounts of personal experiences from other site visitors. There's another link where you can review Mama's tips on how to make pizza, and another where you can browse through Mama's collection of

A Web Page of Your Own

Italian recipes. Before you conclude your visit to this site, be sure to enter the "Mama's Look-Alike Contest." You can't order any of Ragu's products on-line, but I'm willing to bet their retail sales are up as a result of their web site.

Rush Ties—(http://www.rushties.com)

When conservative talk show host Rush Limbaugh started broadcasting his shows on TV as well as radio, he became known for his unique, colorful ties. So many people commented about them and asked where he got them that (good capitalist that he is) he saw a business opportunity and designed his own collection. The response was so overwhelming that he started offering a line of ladies' scarves using the same fabrics, and decorative pocket handkerchiefs as well. Once you leave the home page, you'll be offered links to see pictures of all the tie and scarf collections and prices. If you want a closer look at the colors or fabric designs, all you have to do is click on the tie or scarf in question to get an enlarged picture. Have you ever been at a loss on how to knot a tie or scarf? If you have, try the link which takes you to excellent step-by-step illustrated instructions on each.

Hot, Hot, Hot!—(http://www.hot.presence.com/g/p/H3//)

For some of the coolest hot sauces on the Web, visit the Hot, Hot, Hot! web page. Hot, Hot, Hot! (HHH) sells over 100 types and flavors of exotic hot sauces from all over the world from its specialty shop in Pasadena, California, and through its well-designed web site which makes the most of exceptional color and graphics. The first link offers visitors the choice of seeing products based on name, geographic origin, ingredients, or degree of hotness. In each of these sections they describe in detail what flavor and degree of spiciness and hotness to expect from sauces with names such as "Triple Barn Burner," "Gib's Nuclear Hell," and "Ass Kickin' Hot Sauce." Visitors can also choose among an assortment of gift packages with names such as "Blow Your Head Off

Doing Business on the World-Wide Web

Four-Pack" all of which offer an assortment of sauces based on one of these categories. There's also a section where you can find cookbooks, T-shirts and other food items. Ordering on-line is easy because of the shopping cart system. Buttons which say "Select" are located next to each catalog entry, and automatically record your choices on the on-line order form. There's even a link to help you figure shipping costs regardless of the final destination of your order. If you elect to try any of these products and are hearty enough to live and tell about it, check out Hot, Hot, Hot!'s "Frequent 'Fire' Program" where you can build up points toward free products and other prizes based on how much you buy.

MATIMOP: Israeli Center for R&D— (http://www.Matimop.org.il

With one click of your mouse you can see what's on the cutting edge of technology in fields such as medicine, electronics and biotechnology. MATIMOP, the Israeli Center for Research and Development was developed by the three major Israeli manufacturing associations, and serves as a technology clearinghouse for products developed by Israeli companies and universities. A set of links offers visitors the option of seeing a list of projects available in specific industry areas or searching the entire listing using key words. Visitors can see a one to two paragraph abstract on any project. However, to get more information you have to register using an on-line registration form. When you've registered, all you do in subsequent visits is give your name and password. Then, MATIMOP informs the companies to which the abstracts correspond to send you more information.

Southwest Airlines—(http://www.iflysouthwest.com)

If you'd like to plan a trip without leaving your computer screen, visit Southwest Airline's web site. Your first view will be a home page that looks like a ticket counter, from which you can "take off" to various links. You can check fares and buy tickets on-line, review various vacation packages,

A Web Page of Your Own

or just look through the on-line version of the in-flight catalog. Want to take a trip but you're not sure where? Get information on various cities to which Dallas, TX-based Southwest flies, as well as hotel information which will be useful once you arrive. If you'd like to know more about what types of planes Southwest flies, you can see them by linking to the photo library. Remember those crazy Southwest print and TV ads? You guessed it. You can see some of those, too, in the print and video library of past ads.

Godiva Chocolates—(http://www.godiva.com)

Whether you're a confirmed "chocoholic" or not, you'll like the way Clinton, CT-based Godiva Chocolates has designed its web page. Through a menu designed like the company's trademark gold seal, you'll be offered a series of links where you can: access the on-line catalog complete with easy-to-draw product pictures, review some of the most exotic chocolate recipes you'll see anywhere, find a store near you where you can buy Godiva chocolates, and even enter contests to win a variety of prizes (all chocolate related, of course). If you've ever been offered a piece of candy from a box and had trouble choosing between "the rectangular one with the 'dark chocolate squiggley thing on top' or 'the round one with the white curlicue,' you'll appreciate the section Godiva provides which educates visitors on what to expect from the size and shape of each piece of candy in its boxes. If you've ever forgotten an important birthday or anniversary, you'll also appreciate Godiva's free, on-line "Reminder Service." You give them the dates and they'll remind you of them by e-mail. If your mouth is watering by the time you finish looking around, ordering is easy using the shopping cart method—clicking on the select button next to what you want—and orders are secured on-line.

Security First Network Bank—(http://www.sfnb.com)

Whoever decided bankers have no imagination never visited Security First Network Bank's (SFNB) web page. Many banks have added the Web to

Doing Business on the World-Wide Web

their marketing mix due to the rise in popularity of on-line banking, and there are some superb web pages for banks as a result. However, one of the more innovative of these definitely belongs to SFNB, headquartered in quiet, little Pineville, KY. The three-dimensional bank lobby with the built-in, pictorial web site menu will catch your attention immediately. You can request a complete on-line demonstration of the bank's products and services, and if you're convinced, open an account on-line. If you're not, you can link to a Dave Letterman style list of "Top Ten Reasons You Should Bank With SFNB." If you're just not in the mood to change banks, enter your information in SFNB's guestbook anyway for a chance to win a prize, and don't leave without reading all the stories in SFNB's "Tales from the Vault" link.

Windows '95 Information—(http://windows95.com)

At first, you'll think this web site was developed by Microsoft Corporation to promote Windows '95, and offer helpful tips for using the program. However, this web page wasn't developed by Microsoft, but by Steve Jenkins, a business graduate student at Brigham Young University, Provo, UT. When you visit this web site, you'll surely agree that Microsoft owes Steve Jenkins a big thank you at the very least (if not a nice job offer) for his excellent work promoting Windows '95 for them. Whether you've already upgraded to Windows '95 or are just thinking about it, you'll benefit from connecting to all the links and reading all the news that is news about Windows '95. This site also shows how a little animation can go a long way in "jazzing" up a web page. If you have a sound card, you'll note the various tunes this web site plays as you link to various pages.

Hong Kong University of Science and Technology—(http://www.ust.hk)

Find just about anything you need to know about the Hong Kong University of Science and Technology including: admissions requirements,

A Web Page of Your Own

academic programs available, a campus events calendar, current research projects, and even a faculty directory. Links within the web page lead to an extensive on-line language center, an on-line computer center, and an on-line library. Stay on the home page awhile if you'd like a pictorial tour of campus. The aerial campus photo with the blinking light that you see at the top changes every few seconds or so to show you close-up views of campus buildings and campus scenes.

Fleurtick Flower Bulbs— (http://valley.interact.nl.fleurtick)

The Dutch are world-famous for their beautiful flowers and have made exporting tulip bulbs into a world-wide business. Amsterdam-based Fleurtick BV has surely picked up an even larger international customer base by adding the Web to its marketing mix. Four hyperlinks, each marked by the Dutch national flag, direct you to an on-line catalog which lists the products with accompanying easy-to-access photos, an order form, product information with gardening tips, and a link to Ida Flowers, Fleurtick's counterpart for visitors who want to order flowers instead of bulbs with an option to view the site in either English or Dutch. If you're not sure if a certain type of flower will grow well in your area, try the Fleurtick link with gardening tips to find out more information on sun, water, soil and climate conditions for your choices. Ordering on-line is possible, but both Fleurtick and Ida Flowers caution visitors that the site is not yet secure, and offer alternative ways to order off-line, or explain how to order on-line and transmit credit card information separately.

Arizona Diamondbacks—(http://www.diamondbacks.com)

If you're a baseball fan, you'll enjoy reading about one of the newest major league expansion teams. However, even if you don't know the difference between an RBI and an ERA, you'll still agree that this is a very well-designed web site. Visitors can survey seating options available

Doing Business on the World-Wide Web

and even see a summary of what facilities are available on each seating level before they choose. They can also reserve and purchase individual or season tickets on-line or by following the phone or mail instructions given in the web site. There's even a link which shows the progress on the new stadium construction in downtown Phoenix, AZ and a news/press section where you can keep track of new players the Diamondbacks have signed. Meet the team, the manager and members of the administrative staff in the "Clubhouse," and then surf around the "Team Store" to see if you can find any shirts, baseball caps or other memorabilia you'd like to buy. Here again, there are instructions on ordering over the phone or by mail, but the web site is secure if you want to order on-line. When you return to "Home Plate" (home page), be sure to register for an autographed baseball signed by the team manager before you leave.

A Web Page of Your Own

Section III Review

1. Draw each of the web sites listed in this section. Examine the elements and features of each and make notes of those you'd like to include in your own web page. If you think you'll want to find any of these web pages in the future, put them on your favorites list.

2. Surf the Web and find other web sites with elements and features you like and make notes. Save web sites you especially like to your favorites list.

S E C T I O N F O U R

Planning and Organizing a Web Page

Now that you know how to plan and design a web site and have seen some examples of good design and promotional techniques, let's design a web page. In this section, we'll design a web page for Michael's Publishing, a fictitious company that publishes and distributes business-related books.

Subject Company

Michael's Publishing, Inc. is a medium-sized publisher of business books and workbooks located in the western United States. Michael's sells its books in the United States through major retail outlets (direct and through wholesale distributors), direct to training companies and corporations for conducting in-house training seminars, and through a quarterly catalog in which titles are divided into subject areas such as human resources, accounting/finance, management, etc. Customers can order by mail or by calling a toll-free number. Michael's exhibits most of its titles at trade shows and "bundles" books with compatible software packages written by Apex Software, Inc., a small software development company also located in the western United States.

Michael's is well-known and respected in the American market, but is looking for ways to increase its presence in international markets. Michael's distributes its books internationally to retail outlets direct and through wholesale distributors and will also sell direct to companies, even translating the desired book, if required. Overseas customers also see Michael's exhibit at trade shows and receive the catalog quarterly if they're on Michael's mailing list. However, to place an order, overseas customers need to order by mail from the catalog, call using the regular phone number (since the toll-free number doesn't apply outside the United States), order the book through a local bookstore, or buy it at a trade show.

Planning and Organizing a Web Page

Elements to Include

Given the above information about Michael's Publishing, let's first set up the following on the home page.

1. An e-mail link where customers can ask questions or request information about products directly from Michael's.

2. A guest book where Michael's can ask that users complete a short questionnaire giving name, address, e-mail address, etc. (All names will be added to Michael's customer database and mailing list.)

3. A link to an order form in case users already know what they want and are ready to order without going through the catalog.

4. A link where customers can see a list of specials, new releases and a preview of future releases.

Michael's company logo, address and regular and toll-free phone and fax numbers should appear on every page. (Remember, this won't slow down access time for users with slower modems because once you've drawn a graphic or photo, it can be used again as many times as you want during the same visit without requiring additional draw time.)

What else should be included on the home page? Try to think like both individuals and business customers.

Visualize what will be on the other pages of Michael's web site. Michael's books are available in retail outlets, through its mail order catalog and at trade shows. Therefore, one of the links we designate on the home page should offer customers a list of stores in their area that stock Michael's books. You can do this by displaying a world map and asking the customer to indicate the continent, country, state or province, and city of interest. Then the user can review the list of stores in that area along with locations of each.

Doing Business on the World-Wide Web

Some customers might be interested in visiting Michael's booth at trade shows. So, we should also create a link that displays a list of trade shows where Michael's plans to exhibit, the hotel or convention center where the trade show will be held, the city and country and, if possible, contact information for the person or company coordinating the show.

We can recreate Michael's catalog and offer the option of ordering books on-line. As we set up the catalog, let's remember that it's divided into business subject categories such as human resources, accounting/finance marketing/sales, etc. Since we can be reasonably sure that users will already know what type of book they want, our first link should lead them to a page where they select one of these subject areas. Each area link would then lead to a listing of books in that subject category which could include a picture of each book, a short description of the contents, an order number and a price.

The initial display would have a picture of the book and a one to two paragraph description. For a more detailed description of a book, the user could click on the book or title. We can also offer users the option to see a larger picture of the cover by offering links which enlarge the original picture. (Remember, enlarging the picture will not take an excessive amount of time since the user has already drawn the picture.) Each individual book listing should have a "select" button so the customer can click on it to automatically record it on the order form.

Each subject area section should have a direct link to the order form so the customer can easily access the form to complete other information after making choices. We also need to provide a link on the order form that takes the user back to the list of subject areas in case he wants to order additional books, and one that leads back to the home page. We should also have a link where customers can sign up to receive quarterly catalogs and news of specials and new releases by e-mail.

Provide links at the bottom of each page to give the user the option of going to the top of the current page, back to the beginning page for the

Planning and Organizing a Web Page

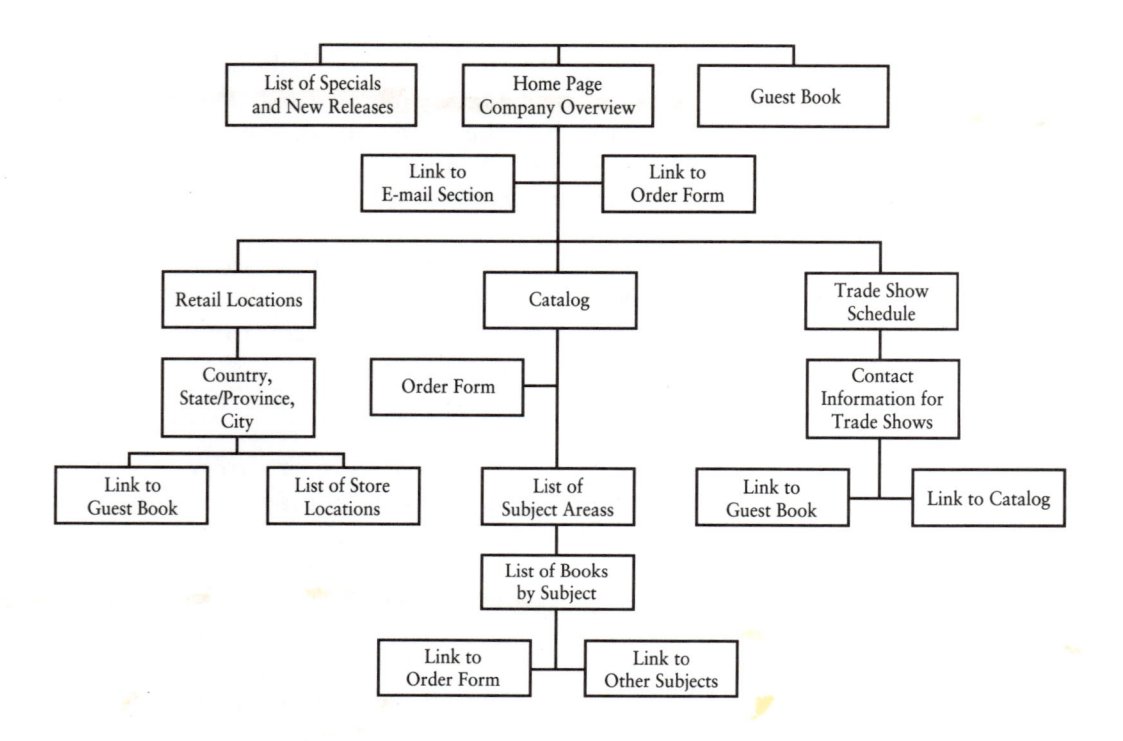

```
                    ┌─────────────┬──────────────┐
            List of Specials   Home Page      Guest Book
            and New Releases   Company Overview
                          │
                  ┌───────┴───────┐
              Link to           Link to
              E-mail Section    Order Form
          ┌───────────────┼───────────────┐
      Retail Locations  Catalog      Trade Show
                                      Schedule
           │             │               │
       Country,      Order Form      Contact
       State/Province,                Information for
       City                           Trade Shows
        ┌──┴──┐          │           ┌────┴────┐
    Link to  List of   List of    Link to    Link to
    Guest    Store     Subject    Guest      Catalog
    Book     Locations Areas      Book
                         │
                     List of Books
                     by Subject
                      ┌──┴──┐
                  Link to   Link to
                  Order Form Other Subjects
```

current section, and back to the top of the home page. A flowchart illustration of how all the pieces fit together is shown above.

Case Analysis

Why did we design our page this way? First, it gives users choices, and everyone likes to be offered a choice. If customers prefer to go to the store to buy the book, Michael's web site offers them a list of stores in their area that would have the books in stock. If they plan to be at a trade show and would like to see if Michael's is scheduled to exhibit, there's a section that lets them check. They can read through an on-line catalog or ask to be on the mailing list to receive future editions in the mail. If they decide to order, they have a choice of doing so by mail,

Doing Business on the World-Wide Web

calling a toll-free number, calling a regular phone number, faxing an order, or ordering on-line.

How can a web site like this help Michael's accomplish its goal of increasing its presence in international markets? Since Michael's has distributors in some countries, its books probably would be available through local bookstores in that country. But how about countries where Michael's doesn't have a distributor? These international customers must order the books through a local bookstore, order by mail from the catalog or visit Michael's trade show booth and buy or order while there. Since the toll-free number doesn't work outside the United States, ordering by phone is inconvenient and expensive. Furthermore, many potential international customers have never heard of Michael's. With a web site, Michael's can communicate with its current customers and attract new ones from anywhere in the world by sharing information and offering convenient options for doing business.

For the future, Michael's should also look into creating links with other web sites to generate even more traffic. Some ideas would include other book publishers' web pages (whose offerings complement what Michael's Publishing offers), training companies, companies which write and/or distribute business interactive software programs, and publishing associations.

Planning and Organizing a Web Page

Section IV Review

1. What are some of the elements you should include in your web site regardless of your company's products or the nature of your business?

2. Draw ITC Golf Tour's web site at *http://www.travelsource.com/golf/itc.html*. What suggestions do you have to improve this web site?

3. Plan and organize a web site for your company. Draw a flowchart to illustrate all hyperlinks, and note where graphics, photos and other creative elements will appear.

Doing Business on the World-Wide Web

SECTION FIVE

Getting Noticed

You're finished designing your web site and it looks perfect! Now, you can't wait to display your web site to all of cyberspace. Whether you did the design work yourself or contracted with an outside firm, you're probably wondering how to find a good, reliable server and how to be sure web surfers can find your web page. Don't worry. Opportunities abound.

Server Strategy

You have a choice of establishing a contract with a server to display your web page or becoming a server yourself. Becoming an Internet server can be an expensive proposition. You need a dedicated, high-capacity T1 or T3 telephone line and the technical expertise and time to maintain it and troubleshoot problems. For most companies, this means a big commitment, usually hiring someone specifically for that purpose, unless present employees can take on the added responsibility.

This is pretty much what happened at Geffen Records, a Los Angeles-based recording company, which decided to invest in its own web server on-site. Geffen went this route because it wanted complete control over what was uploaded and downloaded. The web machine also doubles as the company's mail server, and with the volume of e-mail Geffen receives, the company was assured customers could easily send messages as long as it controlled the server.

Having easy access to the web site has also resulted in many of the employees gaining enough expertise with HTML to update the site. They also use the Internet and Web to track Federal Express packages, send and receive artwork and copy (which saves thousands of dollars), monitor what newsgroup messages are saying about musicians Geffen represents, and scan web pages of fan clubs.

Most companies connect to the Internet on someone else's server. If you contracted with an outside firm to design and maintain your web site,

Getting Noticed

connection to their or another server may be part of your contract. If not, check the business pages of any major newspaper or issues of magazines such as *On-line Access, Internet World* or *NetGuide,* and you'll find plenty of ads from companies with their own servers who will contract to be a server for companies like yours.

Another source to check is "Internet Presence Providers," which you can find by using the Yahoo! search engine. This list contains hundreds of service providers. Ask for quotes and double check what's included in each price. Some charge a flat rate per month and others charge by how many hits you get, regardless of whether these are qualified customers or not.

Check with your Internet service provider or on-line service to see if it provides any special deals for its customers. America Online provides each of its subscribers with two megabytes of space, and both CompuServe and Prodigy provide one megabyte of space to their subscribers.

When you're looking at all the options available to you, it's hard to keep track of all the things you should ask to make sure the server offers all the services you need. Use the following list of questions to help you remember what to ask each provider.

1. *Do you design web pages in addition to implementing and maintaining them?*

    Design services can be costly. You may be quoted widely varying prices and lists of design and maintenance services that may not be included in the price. So, be sure to ask. If you plan to do the design work in-house, make sure the provider understands that you don't need design services included in your quote.

2. *What is included in the set-up fee?*

    These fees are also highly variable, so compare carefully. Remember, there are a lot of ISPs out there, and they all want your business. Don't be afraid to bargain!

Doing Business on the World-Wide Web

3. *Does the fee include domain name registration with the InterNIC?*

All company domain names need to be registered with InterNIC, the body that maintains a list of domain names and keeps track of which names are taken and which are available. It can take up to two months to register a domain name because of the acute demand. Until late 1995, obtaining a domain name was free. Because of the increased demand, it now costs $100 for initial registration plus a $50 annual fee.

4. *What is your speed?*

Server connection speeds range from about 56 kilobyte seconds (Kbs) to 1.54 Kbs (T1 connection) and above. Look for an ISP that has at least a T1 connection. Anything slower will be unacceptable to users even with the fastest speed modems. Before you make a final decision, visit the site at different times of the day and observe how fast the server responds. Be your own judge. If the connection time *seems* slow, it probably *is* slow.

5. *How much disk space do you provide?*

Most providers charge a flat fee for a given amount of hard disk storage. What they provide should be sufficient unless your web page contains a lot of large graphic files. If this is the case, the provider probably has an incremental charge for additional storage space.

6. *Do you charge for network traffic?*

Some providers charge a fee for the data that flows between your web site and those who access it. Most allow a base amount of traffic—about 1.5M bytes per month—and charge for anything over that amount. Some providers will shut down your site if you exceed your traffic allowance by too much (so that your monthly bill won't show excessive charges). Ask if the ISP offers this service. Check whether the ISP charges on a per-kilobyte or per-access basis. Per-kilobyte shows the entire amount of traffic generated, while per-access shows you the number of hits.

Getting Noticed

7. *What utilities and services are provided in the basic subscription price?*

Each web site should have access to basic utilities and services that complement HTML documents. Some providers install basic Common Gateway Interface programs—including a forms-creation package; an image map program that links your site with other pages, database and search engines; and a guest book—that expand capabilities and offer more versatility to users. Ask about having an e-mail mailbox associated with your web page, since this is how customers and visitors can contact you directly.

Other features to ask about include the availability and cost of list servers and auto-responders. A list server lets you send information such as newsletters, product information and specials to everyone on the mailing list. Links can also be provided that automatically add visitors' names to your database after they've registered in the guest book. Auto-responders allow your web site to send out information requested in e-mail messages automatically, which can save you countless dollars in mailing costs.

Many providers charge extra for services such as secure commerce, discussion groups and chat areas. Although you may never need these, or at least not immediately, it's good to know the server has them and what they'll cost if you ever do need them.

8. *What type of usage tracking and reports do you provide?*

Usage tracking helps companies determine who accesses their web sites, what they view and for how long. All ISPs provide a log showing this information, but, oftentimes, it's in a form that is difficult to read and understand. If up-to-the-minute tracking statistics are important to you, ask to see an example of the report the server provides.

Many providers install usage and statistics programs that provide easy-to-read usage statistics. If a server has not done this and has no plans to do so, then you need to customize your own reports.

Doing Business on the World-Wide Web

Search Engines

To be sure everyone cruising the Web knows how to find your web page, connect to or sign up for every search engine or database available. Some are better than others, but your chances of getting the best coverage possible depend on your being accessible to users through as many avenues as possible.

One way to accomplish this easily and efficiently is through two services known as Submit It (*http://www.submit-it.com*) and Promote-It (*http://www.cam.org/psarena/promote-it.html*). Both services work very much the same way. All you need to do is complete a form about your company and your web site. Submit It and Promote-It will then notify the following search engines that you have a new web site: Yahoo!, Starting Point, WebCrawler, EINet, Galaxy, Lycos, Harvest, What's New Tool!, InfoSeek, Whole Internet Catalog, Open Text Web Index, World-Wide Web Worm, Apollo, Jump Station, New Rider's WWW Yellow Pages, The Yellowpages.com, Netcenter, NIKOS and Pronet.

You can also contact Yahoo! directly at *http://www.yahoo.com*, Webcrawler at *http://www.webcrawler.com*, EINet Galaxy at *http://galaxy.einet.net*, and the World-Wide Web Yellow Pages *at http://www.yellow.com/cgi-bin/online/*. American Business Information International will give you a free Yellow Pages listing if you contact them at *http://www.telephonebook.com*.

Register your web site with Excite at *http://www.excite.com* and on the NCSA What's New page, one of the oldest web-based resource guides at *http://www.ncsa.uiuc.edu/SDG/Softeware/Mosaic/Docs/whats-new.html*. This page is sponsored and maintained by the National Center for Supercomputing Applications (NCSA), and provides listings of 200 or more new web sites three times a week.

Register with Open Market's Commercial Sites Index by contacting them at *http://www.directory.net*. Postmaster (*http://www.netcreations.com.postmaster/*) asks you to complete one informational form and then will post your web site to 17 sites free. Posting to additional sites is available for a small charge.

Getting Noticed

You can get a free listing in the International Marketplace, a directory published by American Computer Resources, Inc., which helps businesses attract customers and suppliers among Internet users. Access *http://www.the-acr.com* or send an e-mail message to *lkenny@the-acr.com* for more information.

To be listed in the Webaholics Top 50 Links list, access *http://www.ohiou.edu/rbarrett/webaholics/favlinks/entries.html*. To test how well circulated your web page is, search *http://www.altavista.digital.com* to see if it is registered. If you don't see it, fill out the form provided.

If you'd like to contact traditional publications (newspapers and magazines—remember them?) to inform them of your new web page, access the Electronic Newsstand at *http://www.enews.com* for a list of publications and editors' names.

Newsgroups

Publicize your new web site in appropriate newsgroups. However, don't announce its existence to every newsgroup on the Internet. If you do, you'll receive nasty replies, or "flames" from members of newsgroups where your company or product has no relevance.

You'll find there are newsgroups on every subject imaginable. So, review the list and get involved in a few that are relevant to your company and its products. It's a great way to find out what others in your industry are doing and to keep abreast of market and industry trends. Read some of the posted messages before sending your own so you have an idea of the accepted etiquette of each newsgroup you choose. Once you have a feel for a particular newsgroup, you'll know whether it would be an appropriate place to announce your new web site.

You might even consider including a newsgroup within your web page once you hear what a success it has been for Reebok International, Ltd.

Doing Business on the World-Wide Web

Reebok wanted a presence on the Web for marketing purposes, but also wanted to find out more about what its customers wanted in footwear.

Instead of including just the usual marketing and product information for its product lines, Reebok also included a newsgroup-style conference as part of its web page. In its first nine months on-line, the company received more than 1,200 messages, both positive and negative. Reebok answers all messages on-line—including the negative ones! How's that for effective public relations and customer service?

Reebok's web page averages 250,000 to 500,000 hits per week, and the company is thinking of adding software that will give it more detailed information on who visits the site and why. Reebok launched its web page with a small ad in *Wired* magazine and with a posting to the NCSA What's New page. However, company personnel think that most of the traffic has come as a result of word of mouth. For more information (or to join in a discussion about sneakers and other footwear), visit Reebok's web page at *http://www.planetreebok.com*.

Although newsgroups are usually associated with the Internet as a whole rather than specifically being a part of the Web, it's important to mention that newsgroups can be a helpful business and research tool, sometimes saving you hours of time. Jonelle Kearney, technical writer for Boeckeler Instruments, Inc., a manufacturer of microscopy and video measuring devices for microscopes in Tucson, Arizona, knew little about statistics, but needed to know what symbols to use for mean, standard deviation, and range for an article she was writing. It took five minutes of her time to post her question in the Science, Statistics, Math newsgroup, and she received the answer she needed within hours.

Though this experience made a big impression on her since it probably saved her an hour or two of library research time and travel, she adds that Boeckeler also finds the Internet and World-Wide Web useful as a public relations and marketing tool. For more information on Boeckeler's products or Jonelle's experiences, send a message to *boecklr@primenet.com*.

Getting Noticed

The most important thing to remember when promoting your web page to search engines, databases or newsgroups is that the "one click reaches everyone" approach doesn't work. Take the time to tailor your message to meet the needs or reach the audience of each medium. You'll be happier with the response you receive, and you'll be better able to track the sources of your best responses.

Linking with Other Web Pages

Another way to generate additional traffic is to link with other companies' sites that complement yours. For example, McMillan Publishing has its own web site, but it can also be accessed from a list of publishing companies included in Soundview's web page. Soundview is the company mentioned earlier that specializes in writing and selling summaries of best-selling business books.

Register to be listed in as many industry sites as possible. For example, you can access Barclay's Bank and Wells Fargo Bank by searching for them by name using one or more search engines. However, you can also access them directly from a list of banks that you get when you conduct a search on "banks" or "banking."

If you'd like help finding other companies' web pages to link to your own, take a look at a new service offered by Webconnect (*http://www.worlddata.com/webcon.htm*). This company acts as a broker, finding you appropriate link partners. If both companies agree that the link would be beneficial, the company linked to your web site pays you a monthly fee. According to some users of Webconnect's services, the fees they've been paid by linking partners have paid their server connection bill, with money left over.

Doing Business on the World-Wide Web

On-line Advertising

Since you have this wonderful cyberworld at your disposal, take advantage of its resources to broadcast your new web page. Submit an e-mail description of your web site and URL to "Cool Site of the Day" at *cool@infi.net* and "Spider's Pick of the Day" at *boba@www.com*. Maybe your site will be chosen for inclusion.

Send an announcement about your new web page to the newsgroup *comp.infosystems.www.announce*. You need to include an explanation of your site along with your URL. Create a signature file that promotes your web site so you can attach it to every e-mail message you send. Don't forget to include your URL so people who receive your messages know how to find your web site.

Support Your Web Site in Other Advertising

Advertise and support your web site in your other advertising. Your web page will repay the favor by making your other advertising more effective. Think of it this way: you simply can't convey all the information your customers need in a one-page magazine ad or a 30-second radio spot. However, if you give your URL as part of your ad, customers can find your web site, pick and choose which information they want and send you an e-mail message if they need anything else.

Getting Noticed

Cybermalls

Depending on your product or service, you might want to lease space in a cybermall, or virtual mall, which is a shopping mall on the World-Wide Web. Before deciding to include your site in a virtual mall, ask yourself whether your product or service is something that people would ordinarily go to a mall to buy. If you sell gourmet coffee or discount sporting goods, a cybermall may be the best place for you. However, if you market an industrial product or service, or market to a narrowly focused audience that isn't accustomed to buying from you in a mall or shopping center, think again.

If you decide a cybermall is a good place for your web site and products, you next need to decide on the best location. Think about some of the shopping centers near where you live. They always consist of stores that offer a complementary mix of products and services, and no two stores offer the same thing. This way, each tenant benefits from walk-by traffic from the other occupants. Better locations and larger spaces cost more, and anchor stores (large stores drawing the most attention and customers) pay the most.

The anchor store might be a supermarket or large discount store such as K-Mart or Wal-Mart. You might also find a dry cleaners, veterinary clinic, sandwich shop, video rental store and a florist. Shoppers going to the grocery store might need to rent a video to watch after dinner that evening. When they need a veterinarian or dry cleaners, they know just where to find one. All these products and services complement each other without competing.

Smaller specialty shopping centers might offer stores that fill market niches in the same industry. For example, you might find a specialty shopping center where the anchor store sells furniture and the smaller tenants sell window coverings, carpet and tile, or gourmet kitchen utensils. Developers assume that those who are building or redecorating a home would find it convenient to do all their shopping in one location.

Doing Business on the World-Wide Web

Virtual malls are designed the same way as actual malls. When you're considering whether to lease space in a virtual mall, find out who the other tenants are, especially anchor tenants, and see if their products complement yours. Ask yourself the following questions:

♦ Would buyers of these products buy yours?

♦ Who else is in the virtual mall?

♦ Will they take users away from you?

Wherever you decide to lease space, request a clause in your contract that prohibits the owner from leasing mall space to anyone whose products and services are the same as yours as long as your lease remains in good standing. If you'd like more information on what cybermalls offer and what options are available to you, contact the Multimedia Marketing Group and check their index of Commercial Databases and Malls at *http://hevanet.com.online/com.html*.

Getting Noticed

Section V Review

1. What are the advantages of placing your web site on someone else's server rather than having your own?

2. Is a cybermall the right place for your web site? Why or why not?

3. With which industries would it be beneficial for you to link your company's web site?

4. Name some companies with which you would like your web page linked? Why?

S E C T I O N   S I X

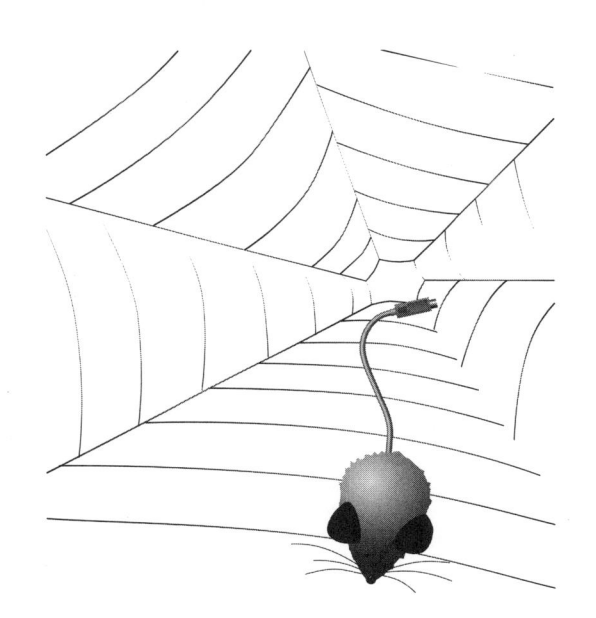

Measuring Success

Ever since the Web started gaining in popularity with companies as an advertising, promotional and marketing tool, on-line advertisers have wondered how they can measure the success of their web page. One obvious way is to track the number of on-line orders your company receives, but what if you don't offer customers the opportunity to order on-line and just give a toll-free number and list of stores? What if customers learn about your company and products on the Web, but choose to buy on location or over the phone instead of ordering on-line? How will you know they first heard about you on the Web?

Getting a Reaction

Don't worry. There are plenty of ways to see how much response your web site generates.

Ask the Customers. Train your employees to ask each customer how they heard about your company regardless of how they place an order. This information will help you gauge how successful your web site is in attracting customers and how successful your other advertising and promotions programs are. To ensure that employees will remember to ask, make it part of the form they use to write up orders.

Offer an Incentive to Order On-line. How many times have you seen a newspaper ad that says, "Bring in this ad and we'll deduct 10% from your purchase," or heard a radio ad that ended with, "Say you heard it on KWEB 95 and get a second item of equal or lesser value free!" You can use the same technique on the Web. Salem Five Cents Savings Bank, Salem, Massachusetts, offers its on-line customers a better rate on CDs and $100 off closing costs on a mortgage. To see how Salem Five Cents Savings Bank promotes these services, access *http://www.salemfive.com/salemfive/*.

Measuring Success

Historical Comparison. Measure the number of hits you receive. Then compare your sales with the last few months and with the previous year's sales during the same month to get a general indication of how much traffic you're getting from the Web.

Monitor Your Incoming Toll-Free Calls. If you urge your on-line customers to call your toll-free number for further information or to order, measure the number of calls you receive based on the previous month's volume and the volume from the previous year during the same month. Some of the difference is probably attributable to the Web. Better yet, if your company has multiple telephone lines, you can list a separate phone number only in your web site and monitor the number of calls you receive on that line.

Offer a Special for On-line Users. Advertise or promote one product or service only on your web site. When customers call or come to your place of business to inquire about that product or service, you'll know they saw it on the Web.

Do I Count "Hits," "Visits," or "Pages?"

Since TV, radio, magazines and direct mail have been around for so long, well-established methods exist for measuring their effectiveness. However, the Web is altogether new territory, and media buyers and advertising sales representatives are still scratching their heads about the best ways to measure the effectiveness of web sites. According to Paul Grand, chairman of NetCount, L.L.C., a web site measuring firm, here are some guidelines to follow:

- ♦ There's a distinction between how many users requested a particular web site, and how many were transferred to it. Request defines a user who wanted access to a web site, but didn't necessarily end up getting it. A transfer means the user actually connected to the site.

Doing Business on the World-Wide Web

♦ Don't measure traffic in "hits." A web site is credited with a "hit" every time a user clicks on one of the graphic components of the site. Therefore, a web page with an abundance of graphics will receive more hits than one with fewer graphics, but it doesn't give an accurate measurement of the web page's actual traffic. "Visits" is also an inaccurate measurement of web site traffic because one user can generate several visits, but is still only one visitor. The most accurate way to compare the amount of traffic among web pages is "pages"—meaning pages transferred. This is the only way to measure how much traffic a web page is *really* receiving unless the company is registering and authenticating *every* user.

Tools and Resources

"Great," you say, "Now I know what to do and what NOT to do to keep track of how effective my web page is. However, I STILL have no idea what tools I need to do it effectively! Aren't there some products or companies out there that can help?"

Many companies now offer products that track usage, visits to and readership of web sites. WebTrack, offered by Webster Network Strategies, Naples, FL, monitors Internet usage, provides statistics and analyzes web site activity. All reports are produced in a graphical format which can be exported to PC-based spreadsheet programs. Contact Webster Network Strategies at *info@webster.com* for more information.

Digital Planet's (Culver City, CA) NetCount (*pgrand@digiplanet.com*) offers a service that provides Web usage figures and statistics with a universal ratings system so vendors can provide advertisers with objective usage statistics. Reports are available on-line or in print to companies that subscribe to one of the company's reporting services.

Group Cortex, Inc. (Philadelphia, PA) (*http://www.cortex.net*) offers Site Track, which allows web page administrators to track visitors and

Measuring Success

optimize web pages so they can add and delete information as needed. Thus, administrators can be sure that the company's web site offers information users want and need.

W3.Com's (Palo Alto, CA) (*http://w3.com*) Personal Web Site Toolkit customizes user information based on registration materials collected on the site and also includes a feature which targets customers to be sent specific e-mail messages based on information gathered while the customer visits the web site.

A. C. Nielsen (Schaumburg, IL), the TV ratings company, formed a partnership with Internet Profiles Corp. (I/Pro) (San Francisco, CA) to provide web advertisers with statistics on response to their own and other companies' web sites. They produce Nielsen I/Pro I/Count, and Nielsen I/Pro I/Audit. For more information, contact Nielsen Media Research at *http://www.nielsen.com* or contact I/Pro at *http://www.ipro.com*.

Three products, Interse's (Sunnyvale, CA), Market Focus (*http://www.interse.com*), net.Analysis from Net Genesis (Cambridge, MA) (*http://www.netgen.com/products/net.Analysis*) and Open Market's, also of Cambridge, MA, Webreporter, offer users the option of generating reports on demand, as well as the ability to customize them. For more information, contact Open Market at *info@openmarket.com*.

Each company has its own report format and design. To see an example of what a report like this looks like, please see the following three pages of NetCount's "Basic Report," "Top Site Pages Report," and "Top 10 Organizations" reports. For more information on NetCount, access *http://www.netcount.com*.

Doing Business on the World-Wide Web

NET COUNT Basic

Prepared for:	Company XYZ
URL:	http://www.companyxyz.com/
Run Date:	April 15, 1996
Report Period:	4/8/96 - 4/14/96

DPOs
Distinct Point Of Origin

	This Week DPO Total* 4/8/96 - 4/14/96	Last Week DPO Total* 4/1/96 - 4/7/96	This Week Daily DPO Average* 4/8/96 - 4/14/96
	25633	25592	4110

DPO Breakdown Of Access By Category

- International: 16.9%
- Unknown: 26.0%
- Commercial: 28.0%
- Educational: 14.2%
- Government: 0.5%
- Military: 0.4%
- Network: 13.7%
- Organization: 0.7%

PITs
Total PITs/% Abandonment

	This Week PIT Total 4/8/96 - 4/14/96	Last Week PIT Total 4/1/96 - 4/7/96	This Week Daily PIT Average 4/8/96 - 4/14/96
	67248/3.81%	71526/4.11%	9606/3.81%

Total Page Information Transfers (PITs) By Day

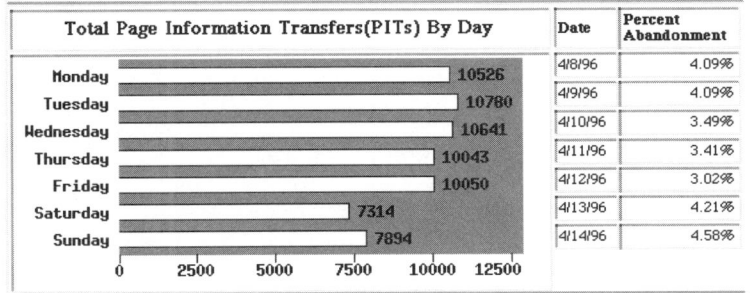

- Monday: 10526
- Tuesday: 10780
- Wednesday: 10641
- Thursday: 10043
- Friday: 10050
- Saturday: 7314
- Sunday: 7894

Date	Percent Abandonment
4/8/96	4.09%
4/9/96	4.09%
4/10/96	3.49%
4/11/96	3.41%
4/12/96	3.02%
4/13/96	4.21%
4/14/96	4.58%

DPO-Distinct Point of Origin
A unique address from which a Browser connects to a Web site on the Internet.

PIT-Page Information Transfer
The successful transfer of the text of a web page to a Browser.

*Does not double count multiple visits by any single DPO.

Abandonment
The percent of requested pages which are not successfully transferred.

*Average based on total daily DPOs, including multiple visits by any single DPO.

Copyright © 1996 NetCount, LLC

Measuring Success

Top Site Pages Report *

Prepared for:	Company XYZ			
URL:	http://www.companyxyz.com/			
Run Date:	April 15, 1996			
Report Period:	4/14/1996			

Document Title / Document Path	PITs / URL Type	%Failure / % Abandoned	Peak Hour -(PST)- / Peak Volume in PITs	Avg Time On Page	Hourly Performance in PITs (Previous Day Shadowed)
Welcome to Company XYZ /index.html	3413 HTML	0.2% 0.3%	4pm 203	141 secs	227
Trees Around the World /Trees/index.html	1100 HTML	0.7% 24.7%	7pm 95	63 secs	95
Italy /cgi-bin/card.cgi	638 CGI	0.0% 0.0%	5pm 56	85 secs	56
Trees Around the World /Trees/Html/loon.html	503 HTML	0.0% 0.0%	5pm 39	67 secs	39
Italy - Pasta /Italy/pasta.html	474 HTML	0.0% 0.0%	7pm 43	75 secs	43
World of Apples /Trees/Html/apple.htm	334 HTML	0.0% 0.0%	7pm 35	52 secs	35
Phones /html/Phones/index.html	212 HTML	0.0% 0.0%	7pm 24	60 secs	24
Greenface /greenface/wow_01.htm	183 HTML	0.0% 0.0%	11am 19	87 secs	19
Wild Roses /Wild/rose10.html	163 HTML	0.0% 0.0%	5pm 19	54 secs	19
Media Services /Media/Html/media.html	143 HTML	0.0% 0.0%	5pm 18	52 secs	18

PIT-Page Information Transfer
The successful transfer of the text of a web page to a Browser.

*This report is not NetCount HeadCount(TM) enhanced.

Copyright © 1996 NetCount, LLC

Doing Business on the World-Wide Web

69

NETCOUNT Plus — Top Ten Organizations by Sub Domain Report*

Prepared for:	Company XYZ
URL:	http://www.companyxyz.com/
Run Date:	April 15, 1996
Report Period:	4/8/96 - 4/14/96

Commercial

#	Domain	Company	BITs	#	Domain	Company	BITs
1.	aol.com	America Online, Inc.	33335	6.	prodigy.com	Prodigy Services Company	2892
2.	netcom.com	NETCOM	10480	7.	pipeline.com	PSI Pipeline	2373
3.	compuserve.com	CompuServe, Inc.	8411	8.	primenet.com	Primenet	2270
4.	ramirez.com	The Ramirez'	7543	9.	erols.com	Erols	1677
5.	gnn.com	O'Reilly & Associates, Inc.	3029	10.	ibm.com	IBM Corporation	1550

Education

#	Domain	School	BITs	#	Domain	School	BITs
1.	berkeley.edu	University of California at Berkeley	2325	6.	umich.edu	University of Michigan -- Computing Center	1395
2.	uiuc.edu	University of Illinois at Urbana-Champaign	1769	7.	vt.edu	Virginia Tech	1375
3.	usc.edu	University of Southern California	1593	8.	umn.edu	University of Minnesota	1057
4.	psu.edu	Pennsylvania State University	1569	9.	uoregon.edu	University of Oregon	1043
5.	ucla.edu	University of California at Los Angeles	1529	10.	ucsd.edu	University of California at San Diego	939

Government

#	Domain	Agency	BITs	#	Domain	Agency	BITs
1.	nasa.gov	National Aeronautic & Space Administration (NASA)	609	6.	loc.gov	Library of Congress	176
2.	nsf.gov	National Science Foundation	248	7.	samhsa.gov	Substance Abuse and Mental Health Services	91
3.	house.gov	House Information Systems	224	8.	usitc.gov	US International Trade Commission	78
4.	nih.gov	National Institutes of Health	199	9.	senate.gov	U.S. Senate Sergeant at Arms	77
5.	lanl.gov	Los Alamos National Laboratory	188	10.	sandia.gov	Sandia National Laboratories	63

Network

#	Domain	Company	BITs	#	Domain	Company	BITs
1.	uu.net	UUNET Technologies, Inc.	5806	6.	att.net	AT&T Easylink Services	1340
2.	earthlink.net	EarthLink Network, Inc.	2870	7.	ibm.net	IBM Advantis Corporation	1248
3.	alter.net	UUNET Technologies, Inc.	2514	8.	idt.net	International Discount Telecommunications	1049
4.	concentric.net	Concentric Research Corporation	1543	9.	infi.net	InfiNet, L.C.	931
5.	mci.net	MCI Telecommunications Corporation	1345	10.	mich.net	Merit Network, Inc.	892

Organization

#	Domain	Organization	BITs	#	Domain	Organization	BITs
1.	cam.org	Communications Accessibles Montreal	273	6.	lafn.org	Los Angeles Free-Net	121
2.	efn.org	Eugene Free Net	196	7.	apc.org	Association for Progressive Communications	119
3.	svi.org	Smart Valley, Inc.	176	8.	michiana.org	Michiana Free-Net Society, Inc.	117
4.	io.org	Internex Online Inc.	131	9.	ets.org	Educational Testing Service	104
5.	mitre.org	MITRE Corporation	131	10.	oclc.org	Online Computer Library Center, Inc.	102

*This report is not NetCount HeadCount(TM) enhanced.

Copyright © 1996 NetCount, LLC

Measuring Success

Section VI Review

1. Name three ways in which you can measure the success of your web site.

2. Of all the methods we discussed for measuring the success of your web site, which one(s) would work best for your company and why?

3. Think of an incentive or promotion you could offer exclusively to Web users so you could track their response separate from other advertising responses.

SECTION SEVEN

Web-Based Business Ideas

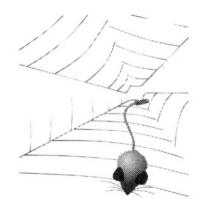

The Internet is becoming a serious place to do business. During 1995, total revenues generated through web sites equaled $436 million. At that point, there were approximately 23,000 companies doing business on the Web and over 6,000 commerical web servers, compared to 588 in late 1994.

The Place To Be Seen

According to Jupiter Communication's "1996 On-line Advertising Report," advertising will become the main source of revenue for companies with web sites. Web revenues in 1995 totaled $43 million, and those from commerical on-line services equaled $12 million for a total of $55 million. They predict that Web and consumer on-line services combined will grow to $343 million in 1996, and to $5 billion by the year 2000, more than twice the amount of radio advertising sales revenues.

From a recent CommerceNet/Nielsen Internet demographics study, about 14% of all Web users, or 2.5 million people, have purchased products on-line. Forrester Research estimates that on-line commerce will account for $31.6 billion by the year 2000, and that $6.9 billion will be from retail sales.

1995 Web Revenues vs. Expenditures for Web Advertising, Site Storage and Site Development

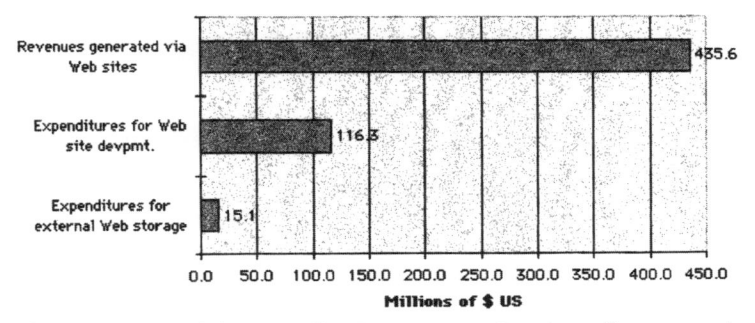

Category	Millions of $ US
Revenues generated via Web sites	435.6
Expenditures for Web site devpmt.	116.3
Expenditures for external Web storage	15.1

Reprinted with permission of ActivMedia, Inc., *reports@activmedia.com* and *http://www.activmedia.com*

Web-Based Business Ideas

ActivMedia estimated total sales on the Web at $118 million between September 1994 and August 1995, and pegged the growth of commercial Web servers from 588 in September 1994 to more than 6,000 by May of 1995. In the time that the Web has experienced meteoric growth, four types of companies have emerged as lucrative strategies for doing business on the World-Wide Web.

- Direct selling of a company's products and services
- Selling advertising space
- Charging fees for accessing contents of a web site
- Charging fees for on-line transactions.

Direct Sales

According to ActivMedia, companies that market products on the Web generated $436 million in sales during 1995, and a company's success in selling products and services on the Web is inversely proportional to the size of the company. Small companies are doing better than large ones, probably because the Web's advantages offer more benefits to a small company than one that already has extensive distribution channels and customer networks in place.

Since the Web is a relatively new marketing and promotions medium, universal acceptance will take time. As a result, although some advertisers have done well, none has reached the one million dollar mark yet.

Some companies do all their business over the Web. Virtual Vineyards, a specialty wine and foods store in Los Altos, Calif. has done thousands of dollars of business solely on the World-Wide Web. In addition to its primary products, Virtual Vineyards includes recipes and a wine matching list so customers can decide which wine is appropriate to serve with their chosen dinner menu.

Doing Business on the World-Wide Web

Peter Granoff, vice president and cofounder, says Virtual Vineyard's website is successful because it offers customers personalized service and specialized information they can't get at retail outlets. Since the store has no physical location, the only way customers can order Virtual Vineyard's products is on-line. Consequently, the biggest barrier to its success has been persuading people to shop and order on-line.

The site averages 1,500 visitors per day and sales are growing by 20% each month. Granoff projects revenues of $10 to $20 million within five years. Granoff's future plans include personalizing the site further by incorporating software that will keep track of customers' likes and dislikes so they can receive personalized shopping tips on-line. For more information, see Virtual Vineyard's Web page at *http://www.virtualvin.com*.

Harley-Davidson, Stamford, CT, mentioned earlier, is not Harley-Davidson's corporate headquarters, but a dealer for Harley-Davidson's products with only 15 employees. Predicting that the loyalty of Harley owners would pay off, the company launched its web site in 1994. They haven't regretted it since. Not only have sales from the web page averaged more than $1000 per week, the company has also received overseas orders from as far away as Singapore and countries of the former Soviet block. The dealership has had no trouble recouping its initial investment. In fact the biggest problem is allocating limited staff time to service the web-generated orders with an already-busy staff. This is only one of the many success stories of how the Web can help a small company increase sales in untapped markets, even with limited resources and distribution channels.

General Electric Company's Plastics Division in Pittsfield, MA, a Web presence since October 1994, uses its web site as an on-line catalog and technical data source for its customers. Although any leads received from on-line users are passed to the sales department for follow-up, none has been connected with any increase in sales. For more information, see GE Plastics' web site at *http://www.ge.com/gep/homepage.html*.

Web-Based Business Ideas

This doesn't mean that marketing on the Internet is ineffective for all large companies, however. During the week before Mother's Day in 1995, 1-800-FLOWERS tallied 600 sales through the company's new web page. Although this amount is only one percent of 1-800-FLOWERS's total on-line sales, the company believes that this increase is significant since its web site was new and many customers didn't even know it existed.

Selling Ad Space

In the fourth quarter of 1995, companies spent about $12.4 million to buy advertising space on the Web according to *Interad Monthly*. By the year 2000, Forrester Research, Inc. forecasts that advertiser spending for on-line media will increase to around $2.6 billion.

To many companies, selling advertising space is a natural extension of their present business. For example, Dealernet, a Lynnwood, WA, company started in March 1994, has generated almost $4 million in revenues displaying classified ads for more than 400 U.S. car dealerships. The company charges a flat fee to include a car dealership's ad in its web site and a monthly maintenance fee thereafter. See Dealernet's web site at *http://dealernet.com*.

Career Mosaic is an on-line classified ad and help wanted database launched by Bernard Hodes Advertising in New York where about 3,000 jobs are listed daily. Users access the site and browse through ads organized by type of work and profiles of hiring companies, which include intricate graphics and photos, as well as text files. Ads stay on the system for 30 days. Career Mosaic has been a tremendous success, generating almost one million dollars in revenues thus far. The largest reason for the success, according to Bernard Hodes, is that the company doesn't pay out half its revenues to buy advertising space. For more information (or if you're looking for a job), see Career Mosaic's web page at *http://www.careermosaic.com*.

Doing Business on the World-Wide Web

Selling Subscriptions

Another way to do a lucrative business on the Web is to charge users a subscription fee in return for instant access to news or information they want or need.

For example, Meredith Corporation (Des Moines, IA) launched an on-line version of its *Successful Farming* magazine, charging $40 for on-line subscriptions. The company thought that this idea would succeed because farmers need current, accurate information on weather forecasts, commodities prices and so forth. The monthly charge is based on agricultural data services such as DTM and FarmData, which charge $25 to $75 per month. See *Successful Farming*'s web site at *http://www.agriculture.com*.

Quote Com, a Reno, NV company, offers subscriptions to its on-line financial databases. The company was started in July 1994 and has generated around $750,000. See Quote Com's web page at *http://www.quote.com*.

On-line Services

Another emerging field for making a living on the Web is charging for a service such as compiling research information or providing space, hyperlinks or other services to clients.

IndustryNet, an on-line marketplace for manufacturers and industrial suppliers, charges companies a flat fee to display and maintain their individual web pages as part of its virtual storefront. The company billed more than $25 million in 1995. IndustryNet doesn't sell on-line, but companies that lease space from them are free to sell their products on-line. In mid-1995, IndustryNet launched an on-line catalog service that lets customers shop for products across its entire web site. Here again, companies pay a flat fee to be in the catalog, which includes monthly site maintenance. For additional information, you can see IndustryNet's web site at *http://www.industry.com*.

Web-Based Business Ideas

Auto-By-Tel, a "no hassle, no haggle" purchasing service for cars, has only had a web page since January 1995. During its first nine months of operation, the company generated 50,000 requests for information, which resulted in more than $300 million in sales of new cars. Auto-By-Tel has more than 1,000 participating dealers and fields 500 information requests per day. If you'd like more information (or are looking for a new car) see Auto-By-Tel's web site at *http://www.autobytel.com*.

Electronic Newsstand (Washington, D.C.,) sells magazine subscriptions on-line. It charges publishers a flat monthly fee for advertising its titles and retains $5 to $10 of each subscription sold. Electronic Newsstand also offers its clients additional options; one allows publishers to sell space to up to 10 advertisers on their home page. Electronic Newsstand has been on the Web since April 1995 and had generated revenues of $250,000 by August 1995. For more information, see Electronic Newsstand's web site at *http://www.enews.com*.

Companies can use the Web to maximize existing operations. The Chocolate Factory, a candy store in Bucks County, PA, established a web page in 1994 to increase its international sales. Besides receiving orders from as far away as Australia, in-store business has increased as a result of people seeing the company's web site. For more information on the Chocolate Factory and its products, access *http://mmink.com/mmink/dossiers/choc.html*.

Douglas Aircraft's customer service department now sells product information and training materials and services over the Web, thus creating a new source of revenues and profits.

Doing Business on the World-Wide Web

Section VII Review

1. What four categories of businesses are proving to be the most successful on the Web?

2. Describe a newsletter or magazine you would like to publish on the Web and charge users for access. Who would be your audience? Why do you think your idea would work?

3. Plan a web-based business where you would sell advertising, much like DealerNet or Career Mosaic. Describe this business and the companies that would buy ads. Who would be your target audience?

Web-Based Business Ideas

SECTION EIGHT

Thwarting Hackers and Cypherpunks

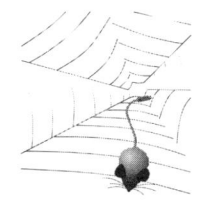

Despite the popularity of the World-Wide Web, two security problems have hindered it from growing more. First, corporations hesitate to allow users access to their files since corporate confidentiality and security might be compromised. Second, users who could make on-line purchases are reluctant to do so because they're afraid their credit card information will be intercepted by hackers. According to a recent study of 415 computer owners by Intelliquest (Austin, TX), 72% of those surveyed would not trust the security of the Internet enough to transmit credit card information.

Concerning Security Issues

Those problems will soon be solved altogether. Firewall programs are now available to restrict access to information, even under the most extreme circumstances. These programs are designed so that the corporate user can "layer" protection (insert separate, overlapping, and redundant layers to create an obstacle to hamper the efforts of cypherpunks) to reduce the possibility that sensitive corporate data, including personnel and payroll data, profit and loss statements and new product testing or liability information could be breached.

However, even the strongest firewall presently available can't protect you against a determined hacker. General Electric Corporation recently discovered a security breach even though it had a substantial firewall protecting the information, and Pipeline, an Internet server, was violated by a cypherpunk group. Firewall programs do work, as long as you use a good program, constantly add new systems and layers, and change passwords often.

W. D. Riley, Data Security Administrator for a National Cancer Research Institute Facility in California, managed the installation of a firewall system and lists the following as important things to remember if your company decides to install a firewall:

Thwarting Hackers and Cypherpunks

- ♦ Plan what goes inside and outside the firewall before you install anything. Also, decide who and what levels of personnel will have access to what information.
- ♦ Test and re-test all connections after you install the firewall.
- ♦ Make a list of restrictions you plan to implement and inform all department heads. Be sure to give them plenty of notice since they will need to brief their respective staffs whether in town or out of town.
- ♦ Give the entire system a test run mid-week before the first weekend it will be in effect so you have time to fix any problems.

For more information on W. D. Riley's experiences installing a firewall, contact him at *wdriley@coh.org*.

Netscape, Internet Explorer and Mosaic have incorporated security support features to accommodate and encourage users to order products on-line. Companies have been working furiously to develop on-line security programs, usually centering around a technology called public key encryption.

Public key encryption works by users encoding their messages with a private key that can be accessed by a public key. Let's say you decide to order a CD-ROM from Egghead Software's catalog. You send a coded and encrypted message to your bank. Your bank then takes the money out of your account, authenticates the message and sends it to Egghead Software with your private key. Egghead receives the note and can verify its authenticity, since it can confirm your bank's public key. It then resubmits the message to your bank and the funds are transferred to Egghead's bank account.

As a result of new innovations such as authentication and public key encryption, Forrester Research reports the Internet will have "close to complete security" by the end of 1996. It further predicts that only one dollar of every $1,000 will be lost to fraud, even when the information is protected, compared to $20 of every $1,000 lost in telephone fraud. Most Internet users agree that given assurance of adequate security, they

Doing Business on the World-Wide Web

would shop and order on-line. In one study, 67% of people in their twenties and 54% of people in their forties said that the Internet will change the way they shop.

Recent improved security and electronic commerce innovations have increased on-line sales, prompting some optimistic projections. According to another study by Forrester Research, world-wide revenues from on-line sales increased from $240 million in 1994 to $350 million in 1995, and could reach $6.9 billion by the year 2000.

Online Transactions

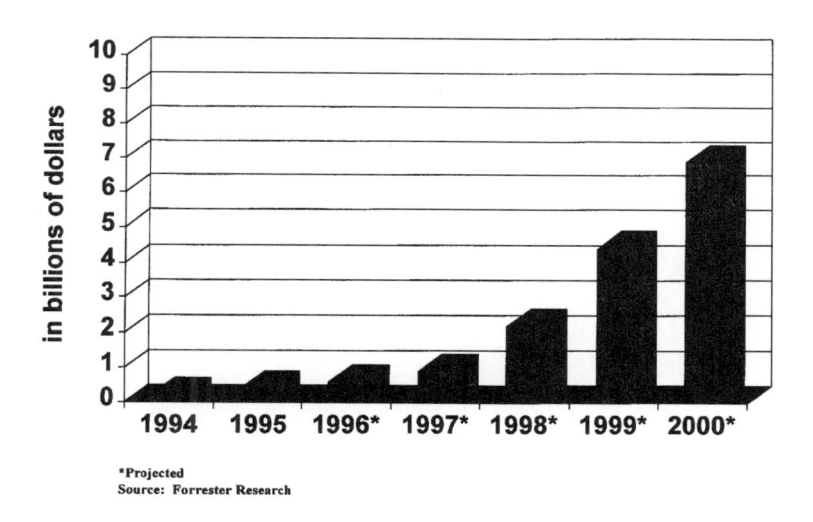

*Projected
Source: Forrester Research

Resources and Tools

Transaction security programs are based on either of two encryption standards, S-HTTP (secure hypertext transaction processing) developed by Terisa Systems (Los Altos, CA) (*info@terisa.com*), and SSL (secure sockets layer) developed by Netscape Communications Corp. (Mountain View, CA) (*http://home.netscape.com*).

Thwarting Hackers and Cypherpunks

These programs had been incompatible, forcing sellers of web browsers and Internet service providers to choose one or the other. However, under a technology partnership agreement, Terisa Systems and Netscape have developed a product that provides security regardless of what service provider or on-line service the user has, and that works with virtually all web browser programs.

Maagnum Resources, Inc. (Cheshire, CT), offers a variety of packages, programs and services such as on-line order processing and credit card authorization to assist businesses that want to encourage customers to order through the company web site. For further information, contact Maagnum Resources at *http://www.maagnum.com.safesite.html*.

Verisign, Inc. (Mountain View, CA) (*info@verisign.com*) has positioned itself as the prime distributor of Internet users' digital identification codes and is backed by companies such as Mitsubishi and Visa International, among others. RSA Data Security (Redwood City, CA), Verisign's parent company, holds the patent on the cryptology technology that underlies both SSL and S-HTTP. Apple, Netscape and Sun Microsystems (Mountain View, CA) have integrated digital identification codes into their software programs. For more information, access *http://www.rsa.com*.

CheckFree Corporation (Columbus, OH) and CyberCash, Inc. (Reston, VA) have cooperated to develop and market products that secure purchases on the Web. CyberCash is a leader in secure Internet payment systems, and CheckFree has developed products for home banking and electronic bill paying. CheckFree licensed CyberCash's security features to create CheckFree Wallet, a program that offers a single solution for electronic payment transactions with checks, credit cards or cash. For more information, contact CheckFree at *http://www.checkfree.com,* and CyberCash at *http://www.cybercash.com*.

Doing Business on the World-Wide Web

The program doesn't require prior registration with merchants and works regardless of which server or on-line service you use. The two companies have also developed a product that can be integrated into any web browser or server.

VISA worked with Microsoft, Inc. to develop a software program to keep credit card transactions private by issuing passwords to customers, and MasterCard worked on a similar system with Netscape. MasterCard also collaborated with IBM, Netscape, CyberCash and GTE Corporation to draft technical specifications for software companies and banks that are developing programs to further secure on-line commerce.

Then MasterCard and VISA combined forces and, after months of negotiation, agreed on a technical standard called Secure Electronic Transaction (SET). GTE, IBM, Microsoft, Netscape, Terisa Systems and Verisign all announced that they would support SET along with the S-HTTP and SSL standards.

Verifone (Redwood City, CA) (*info@verifone.com, http://www.verifone.com*), a manufacturer of point-of-sale credit card readers, has introduced Pay Windows, an electronic payment system that allows customers to make on-line payments with credit cards, debit cards or electronic cash, and Pay Port, a device that hooks up to a computer and reads embedded computer chips within cards. Verifone also acquired Enterprise Integration Technologies (EIT) (Menlo Park, CA), developer of S-HTTP and the founder of CommerceNet. Verifone also made a substantial equity investment in Cybercash. For more information, contact EIT at *info@eit.com*.

Open Market, Inc. (Cambridge, MA) offers Merchant Solution, which includes the hardware and security-supported software needed to launch a Web-based business. The program also includes components that support other business-related services such as promotions, advertising, customer support and secured, on-line ordering. For more information see *http://www.openmarket.com*.

Thwarting Hackers and Cypherpunks

A group of technology companies and several banks has recruited more than 20 companies including Citibank, Bank of America, IBM and Sun Microsystems to develop an electronic check payment system for use over the Internet. The system will require a computer card or "smartcard" that would be fraud-resistant and set off alarms in a case of tampering.

Users would purchase a product on-line and insert the card into their computer. The computer would forward payment with the invoice in a protective, on-line envelope to the merchant. The developers say a prototype will be ready for testing in 1996 and will be set up to handle certified checks and foreign currency.

Does All This Really Work?

Even with all these new innovations, can anyone guarantee that information will always be 100% protected, and that every transaction will reach its destination safely? Probably not. However, most things in life are not absolute. Every time you use an automatic teller machine, you risk that someone will look over your shoulder and memorize your PIN number. We give our credit cards every day to people we don't know, and we give our account numbers to strangers for mail or phone orders. Thus, on-line transactions could actually be more secure than ordering by mail or phone using a credit card. Consider the experience of Robert Silverman, a senior writer for *Inside Media,* a New York-based publication, when he tried to order a wedding gift for a friend by phone, and those of Greet Street Greeting Cards, a company which accepts encrypted orders over the web.

> "A couple of weekends ago, I ordered some outdoor camping gear as a wedding gift for a friend. The couple was registered with a store in Boston, so my ordering travails began with a long-distance call from New York to Boston, during which I read my credit card number to a clerk. The order clerk explained that the item I wished to purchase was only in stock at another outlet, also in New England, so she would have to call there to place my order. And she would also have to call store headquarters in Syracuse, NY, to ensure that my gift had not already been purchased by another wedding guest. How many times was my credit card number repeated up and down the Eastern seaboard? One can only guess. Had I been ordering the gear via the MSN (Microsoft Network) and (retailer) Eddie Bauer, which maintains a virtual storefront, only my order would have been decipherable by the retail chain, with my credit card and banking data read only by the bank."

Greet Street Greeting Cards (*http://www.greetst.com*) has accepted orders through its web site since late 1995. Before the company installed its commerce server, customers placed orders by calling a toll-free number. Two months after installation, the company was doing ten times its previous business volume through its web site, and the phone bills were much lower because of fewer toll-free phone orders.

Greet Street offers its customers the option of using the Web alone, faxing their credit card information, calling a toll-free number, or a combination of all of these. For customers who order over the Web, financial information is automatically transferred from the commerce server into a parsing program with MacAuthorize. The MacAuthorize system sends an e-mail confirmation and the transaction is completed through a separate, totally automated process.

According to Tony Levitan, co-founder of Greet Street, 70% elect to purchase over the Web. He believes that people are much less concerned with security associated with ordering on-line and illustrated this by

Thwarting Hackers and Cypherpunks

recalling an incident where a customer placed an order, and then called the toll-free number with his credit card information. The customer said "You know what? The likelihood that I'm going to get 'ripped off' on-line is less than that I face at a restaurant."

The point is, nothing is ever 100% foolproof, and it never will be. Consumers and merchants can take precautions that will make the process as risk-free as possible. However, there are no guarantees.

Section VIII Review

1. Name the two available encryption programs.

2. Explain how a firewall works.

3. Would you offer customers the option to order from you on-line? Why or why not?

SECTION NINE

The Future
of the Web

Soon, an attractive, well-designed, web site based on HTML won't be enough to impress web surfers. Already, sites are experimenting with technologies that will make video, sound and animation necessary if you want to be noticed and singled out. Already three-dimensional web sites that read Virtual Reality Modeling Language (VRML), HTML's counterpart in the 3-D Web realm, are becoming more common.

Hot Java

If you click on a sound or animation link in a web site you might receive a message such as: "No viewer configured for this file type." This message means your web browser can't recognize or read this part of the web site. Since this is such a common problem, very few web sites are designed to include video, sound or animation.

Sun Microsystems has introduced a program that will make this problem a thing of the past. Sun's program, Hot Java, is written with a language called Java, a hybrid of C and C++ languages, which uses "mini-programs" called applets that your software can download as needed. These applets contain sound and animation readers that enable your web browser to read the sound and animation codes it can't recognize right now. For more information and a demonstration program, see *http://java.sun.com*.

Three-Dimensional Web sites

VRML is the emerging industry standard for designing and navigating 3-D web pages, commonly referred to as worlds. Like HTML, its counterpart in the two-dimensional Web, VRML is the language used to make it possible for web browsers to read the contents of a world.

The Future of the Web

One of VRML's strengths lies in its ability to describe and render complex worlds with very little information. In other words, what you write in VRML won't be that different from what's required in HTML, even though you're working with a third dimension. VRML also provides the means to link smaller worlds together to create larger ones, much like HTML enables users to link from one web page to another.

One of the big problems with VRML, both on- and off-line, has been its lack of speed. VRML is still painfully slow, even on machines optimized for graphics-intensive applications. However, that situation is changing as more VRML viewers become available.

Superscape, a London-based company, has created VisNet, a VRML browser that the company claims is ten times faster than any of the first-generation programs. VisNet works on all Windows platforms and requires at least a 486 computer. It can operate as a stand-alone application or as a plug-in for Netscape and Internet Explorer. For more information, see *http://www.superscape.com*.

Black Sun Interactive (San Franscisco, CA) has introduced Cybergate, a VRML browser with multi-user interaction. This means users, each represented by an avatar (humanoid character), can converse and exchange information with each other while on-line. Cyberhub, the company's server component, enables organizations to create VRML worlds, coordinate users' activities and integrate other VRML worlds. Cyberkit is Black Sun Interactive's product for designing VRML worlds. For further information on all these products, see *http://www.blacksun.com*.

At this writing, Silicon Graphics, Inc. (Mountain View, CA) recently released its first version of the WebSpace viewer for cyber fans who prefer to surf in 3-D. For more information, see Silicon Graphic's web site at *http://www.sgi.com.products*. To see the latest beta version of Worldview, a viewer marketed by Intervist Software, San Francisco, CA, see *http://www.hperion.com.Intervista/worldview.html*. Lastly, a beta version of Live 3D is available for experimentation at *http://www.paperinc.com*. Live 3D was developed by Paper Software, Inc. (Woodstock, NY), which was acquired by Netscape, Inc.

Doing Business on the World-Wide Web

Common Client Interface

Another emerging development is Common Client Interface (CCI), which will supply a means for software applications external to the Internet to work with information on the Web. For example, if you wanted to import data from a web site into a spreadsheet you were working on or into the text of a report, a CCI program that allows your spreadsheet or word processing program to "talk" to the Web would be all you needed to find it and import it.

No longer will we need to recall or reload web pages to see updated information. Browser programs will come equipped with a CCI feature that instructs the page to refresh or update itself automatically with the latest information. To see a demonstration of CCI, draw Autopilot at *http://www.netgen.com/~mkgray/autopilot.html*.

Server Push is a variation on CCI, but it updates information through the server instead of within the browser program. Providing animation within web sites is one of the common uses of Server Push. For more information on Server Push, see *http://www.netscape.com.assist/net_sites/pushpull.html*. For a demonstration, see *http://www.netgen.com* and *http://www.netscape.com.assist.net_sites.mozilla*.

The Many Languages of the Web

As more countries improve phone service and access costs to the Web, customers will demand products that translate the contents of web sites into the language of the user's choice. Spyglass, Inc. of Savoy, IL licensed its Spyglass Mosaic software to Alis Technologies, Inc. of Montreal, Canada. Alis plans to add French, German, Italian and Spanish interfaces and features. To see a demonstration of the French-English version (which is the only one available at this writing), access *http://www.alis.com*.

The Future of the Web

Netscape is working with Globalink (Fairfax, VA) to add enhanced translation features to enable users with Netscape browser programs to access web sites in their choice of available languages. For a demonstration, access *http://www.globalink.com.*

Intranet—Your Company's "Internet within the Internet"

One of the fastest-growing areas of the Internet has nothing to do with the World-Wide Web. Many companies are using Internet-standard technology to establish internal networks called Intranets to enable employees to communicate better within their own offices and with company branch offices, access company information for reports and projects, and work more effectively as a team.

According to Forrester Research, 62% of the companies listed on the Fortune 1000 are using Intranets, or are considering installing them. Here are some of the reasons why:

1. *They solve the problem of information overload.* Instead of sending an e-mail message or written memo to everyone who might be interested, all an employee needs to do is post the message to the company Intranet web page. Then, whoever is interested can read the message there and save it if they want a copy for their files.
2. *Intranets are inexpensive to establish.* If your company has networked PCs, you're already halfway there. Web browsers are cheap, or even free, and server hardware is affordable. Also, the program doesn't have to be introduced all at once to be effective. A company can designate a few departments to "pilot" the system, work out the problems, and then implement it companywide as gradually or quickly as desired.
3. *Intranets are cross-platform.* Most companies have hardware in one department which won't "talk" to the hardware in the next department. Human Resources prefers UNIX, Engineering loves OS/2,

Doing Business on the World-Wide Web

In Conclusion

Marketing and Advertising can't bear the thought of parting with their beloved Macs, and everyone is running some version or other of Windows. Sound familiar? Since an Intranet will work with all these different types of equipment and software, it offers the fastest, least expensive way to get everyone in a company communicating.

4. *The technology is proven.* The Internet has existed for a couple of decades now, even though it didn't receive wide-spread recognition until a few years ago. Therefore, there's been plenty of time to use it and work out any problems. Since Intranets are based on Internet-standard technology, that endurance and reliability are part of the system.

5. *Intranets are fast.* By now, you've done enough web surfing to know that there are videos, animation, and other "bells and whistles" that you'd like to see except it takes too long to download them. With an Intranet, this time lag all but disappears. The "cool" video that would take eight minutes to download with your 28,800 bps modem (or about 20 minutes with your 14,400 bps modem), takes seconds to download on an Intranet.

Companies are only just beginning to discover how useful Intranets are. Some are even starting to make the information available to customers as well as employees. A good example is Federal Express (*http://www.fedex.com*) which has made it possible for customers to trace their own packages on-line. If more people become accustomed to doing this instead of calling the toll-free number, think of how much money Federal Express saves in telephone charges and employee time.

Plugs-Ins—for an even flashier Web

When Netscape, Microsoft, Mosaic, and other developers of web browsers introduced their programs, they never could have predicted that web site developments and capabilities would soon surpass what their browsers could offer users. Enter developers of plug-ins, or add-on programs that let users view intricate graphics, videos, animation, 3-D

The Growing U.S. Market for Internet Tools

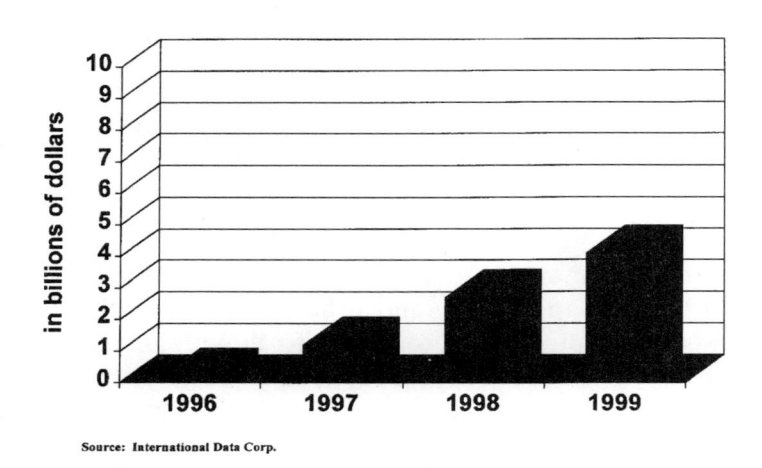

worlds, and so on. With the Web developing at such a quick rate, the market for plug-ins and other Internet tools is projected to skyrocket over the next few years.

At this writing, here are some of the plug-ins available to you free from *PC Computing's* web site (*http://www.pccomputing.com*), or by accessing the developer's site. Most of these were developed for Netscape 2.0 and later versions. However, by the time you read this, Microsoft's Internet Explorer 3.0 and higher will also support all these and any future plug-ins developed for Netscape.

Macromedia Shockwave. Do you want to view two and three-dimensional animation, streaming audio and video files, and special effects files. This is what you need. For more information and a demonstration, see *http://www.macromedia.com*.

Adobe Acrobat Amber. Lets you produce graphically-rich documents in any word processor, spreadsheet or desktop publishing program, and then

Doing Business on the World-Wide Web

convert the file to portable document format (PDF) for viewing. For more information, see Adobe's web page at *http://www.adobe.com/amber.*

Formula One/Net. This is what you need if you want to put "live numbers" in your web site. An example of live numbers would be an interactive spreadsheet or simple financial model where users could calculate their own mortgage amortization, or projected earnings on a particular stock. For more information, see *http://www.visualcomp.com.*

Live 3-D. Experience the best of 3-D VRML worlds. In fact, Netscape liked this one so much they decided to buy it. Veteran users will tell you that it's a little hard to get used to at first, but well worth it. For more information, see Netscape's web page at *http://home.netscape.com/comprod/products/navigator/live3d.*

RealAudio. Have you ever wanted to know what a sound file sounds like while it's downloading? Do you want to find out? RealAudio plays sound files in streaming audio, which sacrifices sound quality for convenience (think AM radio). However, it's perfect for applications such as speeches or sporting events where sound quality isn't crucial. RealAudio also offers built-in forward, rewind, pause and volume controls. For more information, and a list of sites that will work with RealAudio, access *http://www.realaudio.com.*

Web Translator. Now you can "Parlez Francais" or "Sprechen Deutsche" with a click of your mouse. Web Translator can convert the text of a web page from French, German or Spanish to English or vice versa. For more information, see Globalink's web site at *http://www.globalink.com.*

CoolTalk. Want to talk to another computer user? CoolTalk lets you hold an audio conference with your computer. A recording feature, mute button, freehand drawing tool which works with a digitizing tablet, and magnification tool are also useful. For more information, access *http://ice.insoft.com.*

The Future of the Web

Talking on the Computer?

Move over Ma Bell! The first software programs that will enable us to talk on the computer as we do now on the telephone are on the market. The best news is you can talk to anyone, anywhere, anytime for the cost of a call to your local access Internet provider. Can't you already hear your long distance provider screaming?

The way these programs work is by audio compression technology, which has become good enough and fast enough to compress and digitize your voice as you speak. Then, it breaks it up into packets and sends it over the Internet. At the other end, another machine reassembles the packets and plays your reconstructed voice to the person you're talking to.

At this stage, there are still many glitches to be worked out. Some products require you to call their server to schedule even the simplest connection. Sound quality varies from near telephone quality to barely understandable, and there's an obvious time delay with all the products. Furthermore, none of the products presently available is compatible with the others. So, if you don't have the same software product handling both ends of the call, you're out of luck—for now anyway. Expect things to change very fast, and quality to improve. In the meantime, if you want to be one of the trailblazers, take a look at the following software programs: Internet Phone (*http://www.vocaltec.com*), DigiPhone (*http://www.planeteers.com*), WebTalk (*http://www.qdeck.com*), CyberPhone (*http://www.magenta.com*), WebPhone (*http://www.itelco.com*), CoolTalk (*http://www.insoft.com*), and Televox (*http://voxware.com*).

Virtual Meeting Rooms

For your next out-of-town meeting, you might not need airline tickets or hotel reservations. You won't even need to leave your office! There are now software programs available which will enable groups of more than two people to hold meetings over the Internet. For an example of this

Doing Business on the World-Wide Web

type of program, take a look at Microsoft Corporation's NetMeeting on Microsoft's web page (*http://www.msn.com*). Unlike the Internet phone programs mentioned previously, NetMeeting is based on international standards, so there is no compatibility problem. NetMeeting allows participants to transfer files by modem, write ideas or sketch designs on a "whiteboard" which comes as part of the program, and even refer to things written or drawn on the board by pointing at them such that others in the group can see. Another meeting/conference program is CU-See Me by White Pine Software, Nashua, NH. Like NetMeeting, CU-See Me allows more than two people to conduct a meeting over the Internet, and includes a "whiteboard," and allows file transfers.

Section IX Review

1. Draw the demonstration sites for Hot Java, Common Client Interface and Server Push to see how these new features will work.

2. Draw the web pages for WebSpace, WorldView and WebFX to see how VRML works. Would your web site benefit by being three-dimensional? Why or why not?

3. Draw the web sites for at least two of the plug-ins which sound interesting to you.

In Conclusion

During a panel discussion at Comdex, the computer industry's largest trade show, the moderator asked the audience of 200 systems administrators how many of their companies had a presence on the Web. About 50 attendees answered affirmatively. Immediately, everyone's attention shifted from the panel discussion to those 50 people.

Although some minor technical problems must still be worked out, no one can ignore the impact the Web has had on the way business is transacted. Companies created more than 60,000 web sites in 1995, which contained information as diverse as the latest crop prices to the platforms of Russian political candidates. Many companies already consider that creating a presence on the Web is just a part of modern business, and many others have discovered that their Web presence is good for business.

The Web has experienced explosive growth, and this is just the beginning. Remember, progress is seldom made without leaving somebody behind. Don't let it be you! If you aren't on the Web now and don't have plans to be, you may want to reconsider. In all probability, your competitors are.

Resource Directory

Books

Angell, David, and Brent Heslop. *The Internet Business Companion: Growing Your Business in the Electronic Age.* Reading, MA: Addison-Wesley Publishing, 1994.

Cook, David, and Deborah Sellers. *Launching a Business on the Web.* Indianapolis, IN: Que Corp., 1995.

Cronin, Mary J. *Doing Business on the Internet.* New York: Van Nostrand Reinhold Publishing, 1995.

Cronin, Mary, *The Internet Strategy Handbook.* Cambridge, MA, Harvard University Press, 1996.

Downing, Paul, and Thomas Kuegler and Joshua Testerman, "*Web Advertising and Marketing,*" Prima Publishing, 1996.

Ellsworth, Jill, and Matthew Ellsworth. *Marketing on the Internet.* New York: John Wiley & Sons Publishing, 1995.

Fahey, Mary Jo. *Web Publisher's Design Guide for Mac Users.* Scottsdale, AZ: Coriolis Group, 1995.

Gilster, Paul. *Finding it On the Internet.* New York: John Wiley & Sons Publishing, 1995.

Gilster, Paul. *The Mosaic Navigator.* New York: John Wiley & Sons Publishing, 1995.

Graef, Jean. *Leveraging Know-How.* City, State: Montague Institute, 1996.

Graham, Ian S. *HTML Sourcebook.* New York: John Wiley & Sons Publishing, 1995.

Kalakota, Ravi and Andrew Whinston, "Frontiers of Electronic Commerce," New York: Addison-Wesley, 1996.

Jannsa, Kris and Ken Cipe, "World-Wide Web Directory," Jamsa Press, Las Vegas, NV. 1995.

LeMay, Laura. *Teach Yourself Web Publishing With HTML in a Week.* New York: SAMS Publishing, 1995.

Levine, John R., and Carol Baroudi. *The Internet for Dummies.* New York: IDG Books Worldwide, Inc., 1994.

Levinson, Jay C., and Charles Rubin. *Guerrilla Marketing On-Line.* New York: Houghton Mifflin Publishing Co., 1994.

Lynch, Daniel C., and Leslie Lundquist. *"Digital Money, the New Era of Internet Commerce,"* New York: John Wiley & Son Publishing, 1996.

Morris, Mary E. S. *HTML for Fun and Profit.* New York: Prentice-Hall Publishing, 1995.

Stein, Lincoln, D. *How to Set Up and Maintain a World-Wide Web Site.* Reading, MA: Addison-Wesley Publishing Co., 1995.

Tapscott, Don, "The Digital Economy," New York: McGraw-Hill, 1996.

Weaver, Mike, and Ed de Presno. *The On-line World: How to Profit from the Information Superhighway.* New York: Productive Publications, 1994.

Magazines

On-Line Access
5615 W. Cermak Rd.
Chicago, IL 60650-9884
800-366-6336

Internet World
Mecklermedia
Westport, CT
iwsubs@kable.com

Interactive Week
P.O. Box 10506
Riverton, NJ 08076-0506
http://www.interactive-week.com/intweek

Net Guide
600 Community Drive
Manhasset, NY 11030
800-829-0421
e-mail *crenta@comp.com* or *http://techweb.cmp.com/net*

New Media
901 Mariners Island Blvd., Ste. 365
San Mateo, CA 94404
415-573-5170
http://www.hyperstand.com

Seminars

The Basics of the Internet, Padgett-Thompson, a division of American Management Association, P.O. Box 410, Saranac Lake, NY 12983-0410, 800-255-4141

Resource Directory

Doing Business on the Internet, Skill Path Seminars, P.O. Box 2768, Mission, KS 66201-2768, 800-873-7545, 913-362-4241 (fax), *skillpath@mcimail.com* or *7293072@mcimail.com*

Doing Business on the Internet, Data Tech Institute, P.O. Box 2429, Clifton, NJ 07015, 201-478-5400, 201-478-4418 (fax), *http://www.datatech.com*

Finding It on the Internet, Skill Path Seminars, P.O. Box 2768, Mission, KS 66201-2768, 800-873-7545, 913-362-4241 (fax), *skillpath@mcimail.com* or *7293072@mcimail.com*

How to Build Your Business on the Internet, National Seminars Group, a division of Rockhurst College Continuing Education Center, Inc., P.O. Box 2949, Shawnee Mission, KS 66201-1349, 800-258-7246, *rccec@accunet.com*

How to Understand, Access and Use the Internet, Fred Pryor Seminars, a division of Pryor Resources, Inc., P.O. Box 2951, Shawnee Mission, KS 66201, 800-255-6139, 913-722-8585 (fax)

Mastering the Internet, Caldwell Consulting Associates, P.O. Box 29143, Richmond, VA 23242-0143, 804-740-2469, 804-740-0335 (fax), *info@caldwell.com*

Web Browser Programs

Cyberjack 7.0—Symantec Corp., Delrina Group, *http://www.delrina.com*

Emissary 1.1—Wollongong Group, *http://www.twg.com*

Explore Anywhere 2.0—FTP Software, *http://ftp.com*

Internet Explorer 3.0—Microsoft Corp., *http://www.microsoft.com*

Doing Business on the World-Wide Web

Internet/Mosaic in a Box 2.0—CompuServe, Internet Division, *http://www.spry.com*

NCSA Mosaic—University of Illinois, *http://www.ncsa.uiuc.edu*

Netscape Navigator 2.0—Netscape Communications, *http://home.netscape.com*

PowerBrowser—Oracle Corp., *http://www.oracle.com*

Spyglass Mosaic 2.1—Spyglass, Inc., *http://www.spyglass.com*

WebExplorer Mosaic 1.03—IBM, *http://www.raleighibm.com*

WebSurfer—Net Manage, Inc., *http://www.netmanage.com*

Web Page Design Software

All-in-One Web Surfing and Publishing Kit—Coriolis Group, *http://www3.primenet.com/coriolis*

Front Page—Microsoft Corp., *http://www.microsoft.com*

Hot Dog—Sausage Software (Anawave Software), *http://www.sausage.com*

HoTMetaL Pro—Softquad, Inc., *http://www.sq.com/products/hotmetal/hmp-org.htm*

InContext Spider—InContext Systems, *http://incontext.com*

Internet Assistant—Microsoft Corp., *http://www.microsoft.com*

Internet Publisher—Novell, Inc., *http://wp.novell.com/elecpub/inpub.htm* (requires at least WordPerfect 6.0 for Windows)

Resource Directory

Internotes Web Publisher—Skisoft, Inc., *http://www.skisoft.com.skisoft*

Navipress—Navisoft, Inc., *http://www.navisoft.com*

Page Mill—Adobe, Inc., *http://www.adobe.com* (Mac only; Windows version due for release mid-1996)

WebAuthor 2.0—Quarterdeck Office Systems, *http://www.qdeck.com* (requires at least Word 6.0)

Web Wizard: The Duke of URL—Arta Software, *http://www.halcyon.com/Webwizard/welcome.html*

Web Series—SBT Internet Systems, *http://www.sbt.com*

Glossary

Terminology

Here's a list of the more commonly used terms associated with the Web and the Internet.

Access	To request your browser to find a specific web site. Also called draw.
Avatar	A graphic character, usually in human form, adopted by a user to explore a 3-D (VRML) web site (or world).
CCI (Common Client Interface)	Enables use of software programs external to Internet to interact with web browser programs.
CGI (Common Gateway Interface)	Enables communication between two dissimilar networks.
Cruising	Another term for browsing the Internet, or Web. Also called surfing.
Cybermall	A web page on which companies buy space to sell their products and services. Also referred to as a virtual mall.
Cypherpunk	Someone who tries to acquire access to unauthorized or secured information on the Internet. Also referred to as a hacker.
Database	See Search Engine.
Dead End	A page or portion of a web site with no information because it's "under construction."

Glossary

114

Decryption	Technique used in unscrambling an encrypted message, usually with a key.
Draw	See Access.
Draw time	Time needed for modem and web browser software to access all elements of web page from servers.
e-mail (Electronic Mail)	Communicating with someone by sending a message by computer.
Encryption	Technique used in security software that scrambles credit card numbers and other confidential information for transmission over the Web. See also S-HTTP and SSC.
Firewall	Feature of security software that protects credit card numbers and other confidential information from hackers.
GIF (Graphical Interchange Format)	Universally supported format for graphics used in web sites, especially graphs and line art.
GIF89a	A superset of GIF. Allows an image to have areas that are assigned to disappear and show through to another background image to create the illusion that the image is floating.
GUI (Graphical User Interface)	A program that enables users to view files and work with them in a graphic environment (i.e., Windows, Macintosh or OS/2).

Doing Business on the World-Wide Web

Guest Book	Feature included on first page of many web sites that asks visitors to fill out a form with their contact information.
Hacker	See Cypherpunk.
Hits	Measurement for how many users and potential customers accessed your web page. See also Visits.
Home Page	First page of any web site that usually provides an introduction and key words, which act as links to further information.
Hotlist	Feature that acts as a "bookmark," allowing user to create a file of frequently accessed web sites.
Hyperlink	Highlighted word, phrase or graphic within a web page, which accesses additional data when you click on it with your mouse. Also called a link.
Hypermedia	Ability to use different media (animation, sound, graphics, etc.) in designing a web page.
Hypertext	Data that provides links between key elements in web pages. Allows user to access and view information in any order.

Glossary

HTML (Hypertext Markup Language)	Language used to write web pages and create links that enable the user to access additional information.
HTTP (Hypertext Transport Protocol)	Makes web browsing possible by clicking the mouse on links established within a web page. The beginning of every web site address.
Intranet	Internal use of the Internet and the Web, usually at large companies with multiple locations. Designed to incorporate a combination of voice, video and data to help employees, communicate with other offices, research data for reports and projects, and work in teams and groups.
ISP (Internet Service Provider)	An organization that provides users access to the Internet.
JPEG (Joint Photographic Experts Group	A compression technique that reduces a graphics file by as much as 96%. Especially useful for photo files.
Link	See Hyperlink.
Modem	Communications device that transmits data between single computers, Internet servers and on-line services.
Newsgroups	Internet message areas that serve groups with specific interests.

Doing Business on the World-Wide Web

Plug-in	An application such as video, sound or 3-D viewing which can be added to a web browser supported by Netscape 2.0 and Internet Explorer 3.0.
PPP (Point-to-point protocol)	A type of Internet access that gives you virtually direct access to the Internet.
Private Key	What a receiver uses to decrypt a message. See also public key.
Public Key	What a sender retrieves (usually published in universally-accessible database) to encrypt a message.
S-HTTP (Secure Hypertext Transaction Processing)	One of two leading encryption techniques used to protect confidential information while it is transmitted over the Web.
SSL (Secure Sockets Layer)	Another leading encryption technique used to protect confidential information while it is transmitted on the Web.
Search Engine	Tool or command that enables you to locate information within the Web or access it from a remote computer e.g., Gopher, GNN, Yahoo!, Webcrawler, WWW Worm, Telnet, etc.).
Server Push	New feature that instructs a server to update information on a previously drawn web page.
SET (Secure Electronic Transaction)	Newest encryption technique used to protect confidential information on the Web.

Glossary

Shell Account	An account with an ISP that provides basic access to the Internet. Usually includes access to text files only.
Shopping Cart	A web page design feature which enables users to order items without having to go back and forth to the order form page.
SLIP (Serial Line Internet Protocol)	A direct type of Internet access account that requires TCP/IP software.
Surfing	Another term for browsing the Internet, or Web. Also called cruising.
T1 or T3 Line	High-bandwidth, leased telephone lines used to connect local area networks (LANs) to the Internet.
TCP/IP (Transmission Control Protocol/Internet Protocol)	A series of "rules" that computers follow to communicate across the Internet.
Uniform Resource Locator (URL)	Mechanism for locating a specific web page by giving its address.
Viewer	Same as Web browser, but for three-dimensional environments.
Visits	Measurement for how many users and potential customers accessed your web page and links. Seen by many as a more reliable measure of response than counting the number of hits. See also Hits.

Doing Business on the World-Wide Web

Virtual Mall	See Cybermall.
VRML (Virtual Reality Modeling Language)	The language used to create links in three dimensional web sites (worlds).
Web Browser	Generic term for any software program that enables users to navigate the Web.
Web Page	Page about a company or subject usually connected with additional pages, graphics and pictures with hyperlinks, or links within text. Also referred to as a web site. The two terms are used interchangeably throughout this book.
Web Site	See web page.
Whiteboard	A feature associated with an Internet meeting program which allows participants to write things that the others can see as they would on a blackboard in a physical meeting room.
World	Three-dimensional web site.

Glossary

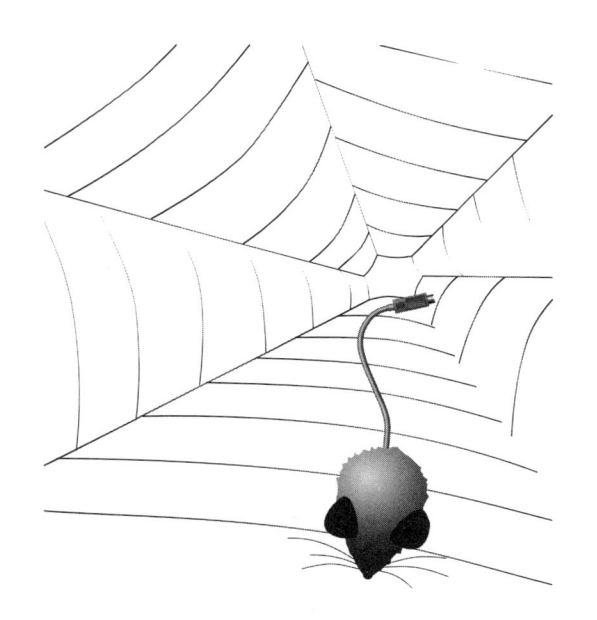

References

Amdur, Dan. "The Scene is Set for Multimedia on the Web," *NewMedia,* November 1995, pp. 42–52.

Anderson, Howard. "Showdown Over E-Cash," *Upside,* January 1996, p. 32.

Arnold, Stephen E. "The Key to Security," *Upside,* April 1996, pp. 78–88.

Asbrand, Deborah, "Technology: The Best Defense," *Information Week* June 3, 1996, pp. 61–64.

Ayre, Rick, and Thomas Mace. "Just Browsing," *PC Magazine,* March 12, 1996, pp. 100–148.

Barr, Christopher. "All You Need to Go On-line," *PC World,* June 1995, pp. 121–148.

Borsook, Paulina. "Demolition Man," *Network World,* September 1995, pp. 27–30.

Bort, Julie. "Should Your Company Have a Web Site?" *Client/Server Computing,* September 1995, pp. 55–58.

Bournellas, Cynthia. "Internet '95," *Internet World,* November 1995, pp. 47–56.

Callahan, Steven E. "Web Site on a Budget," *Internet World,* April 1996, pp. 55–61.

Calloway, Erin, "Intro to Intranets," *PC Week,* June 3, 1996, E16.

Crichton, Michael. *Disclosure.* New York: Ballantine Books, pp. 42–45.

Cushman, Jennifer. "Advertising in Cyberspace," *Tuscon Citizen,* pp. 1, 8.

References

Cutler, Matthew, and Matthew Gray. "The Parrallax View," *Internet World,* July 1995, pp. 30–32.

Davis, Susie, and Andrew Kantor. "Internet News," *Internet World,* July 1995, pp. 14–15.

Dern, Dan. "The Running Dogs of Net.Capitalism," *Net World,* September 1995, pp. 7–8, 11–14.

Elgan, Mike, "Love the Web? Now You Can Build Your Own," *Windows Magazine,* pp. 47–48.

Engleman, Linda J. "Strut Your Stuff," *Internet World,* January 1996, p. 87.

Fitzgerald, Nora. "Generating Traffic on the Information Superhighway," *World Trade,* March 1996, pp. 80–81.

Frook, John E. "Truly a World-Wide Web," *Communications Week,* November 6, 1995, p. 45.

Frook, John E. "Web Add-On Help Identify Site Visitors," *Communications Week,* October 30, 1995, pp. 27–28.

Frook, John E. "Web Site Demographics," *Interactive Age,* a supplement to *Communications Week,* September 25, 1995, pp. 1A, 12.

Gaffin, Adam. "Hello—Is Anyone Out There?" *Network World,* September 1995, pp. 33–34.

Galifianakis, Nick. "Wired, Wary of On-Line Shopping," *USA Today,* November 13, 1995, p. 8E.

Gibbs, Mark. "Piling Up the Virtual Money," *Network World,* September 1995, pp. 17–22.

Doing Business on the World-Wide Web

Gibbs, Mark. "The Millennium Bandwagon," *Network World*, September 1995, p. 38.

Gilster, Paul. "The Internet Made Easy," *CompuServe Magazine*, June 1995, pp. 12–25.

Gilster, Paul. *The Mosaic Navigator.* New York: John Wiley & Sons Publishing, 1995, pp. 24–26.

Goldsmith, Neal. "Doing Business on the Net," Tribeca Research, New York, 1995, pp. 50–59.

Gregston, Brent. "The Internet: A Global Look," *Internet World*, November 1995, pp. 95–101.

Hwang, Diana. "Page Proof: Rating Sites on the World-Wide Web," *Reseller Week*, August 28, 1995, p. 8.

Internet Business Advantage. "Decrypting Encryption Terminology," June 1996, p. 9.

Internet Business Advantage, "SoftCart Makes On-line Shopping a Breeze," June 1996 p. 5–6.

Kantor, Andrew. "Jack in and Geek Out," *Internet World*, July 1995, pp. 26–28.

Kantor, Andrew. "Ladies and Gentlemen, Start Your Engines," *Internet World*, September 1995, pp. 16–18.

Kantor, Andrew, and Tristan Louis. "Internet News," *Internet World*, September 1995, pp. 12–14.

Karpinski, Richard. "Virtual Reality Web Site Introduced," *Communications Week*, November 6, 1995, p. 5.

References

Lawton, Stephen. "The Intranet Grows Up," *Digital News & Review,* June 1996, p. 4.

Lee, Lydia. "On-line News," *NewMedia,* November 1995, p. 26.

Maddox, Kate, Mitch Wagner, and Clinton Wilder. "Making Money on the Web," *Information Week,* September 4, 1995, pp. 31–40.

Mendelson, Edward. "Publish to the Web: No Experience Required," *PC Magazine,* October 10, 1995, pp. 205–216.

Mullich, Joe. "Schlumberger's Self-Serve Intranet," *PC Week,* May 27, 1996, pp. 48–50.

Olson, Jeff. "Not Yet Caught in the Web," *http://www.summary.com,* pp. 1–5.

Radosevich, Lynda, "Internet Plumbing Comes to Groupware," *Datamation.* May 15, 1996, pp. 58–62.

Rafter, Michelle V. "A Home of Your Own," *On-Line Access,* September 1995, pp. 46–53.

Randell, Nell, "Net Essentials: See What You've Been Missing on the Web," *Internet World.* May 1996, pp. 58–59.

Raynovitch, R. Scot. "Building a Firewall for ATM," *LAN Times,* October 23, 1995, p. 38.

Reichard, Kevin. "A Site of Your Own," *PC Magazine,* October 10, 1995, pp. 227–238.

Resnick, Rosalind. "Follow the Money," *Internet World,* May 1996, pp. 34–36.

Richardson, Eric. "Site Construction," *Internet World,* April 1996, pp. 62–66.

Doing Business on the World-Wide Web

Rigdon, Joan. "Blame Retailers for Web's Slow Start as a Mall," *Wall Street Journal,* September 28, 1995, pp. B1, B4.

Riley, W. D. "Behind the Wall," *Datamation,* May 15, 1996, p. 33.

Robertson, Niel. "WWW: The Next Generation," *Internet World,* November 1995, pp. 34–37.

Rose, Harrison M., "Doing Business In Cyberspace," *New Media,* April 22, 1996, pp. 30–34.

Rupley, Sebastian, "Digital Bucks Stop Here," *PC Magazine,* May 28, 1996, pp. 54–60.

Sabo, James. "Build a Better Web Page," *NetGuide,* November 1995, pp. 70–75.

Sandberg, Jared. "Electronic Check Payment Plan for the Internet to be Developed," *Wall Street Journal,* October 12, 1995, p. B7.

Sandberg, Jared. "Mastercard, Backed by IBM and Others Enters Fight for Internet-Payment Rules," *Wall Street Journal,* October 14, 1995, p. B9.

Santalesa, Richard. "Simply Hyperactive," *NetGuide,* August 1995, pp. 63–67.

Sauzeau, Ben. "Web Ads: Tricks and Traps," *http://www.zram.com,* pp. 1–5.

Schmit, Julie. "Virtual Stores Open Doors," *USA Today,* November 13, 1995, p. 8E.

Selingo, Jeff. "Clients Swarm World-Wide Web," *Arizona Republic,* July 12, 1995, pp. D1–2.

References

Selingo, Jeff. "Smart Shoppers Follow Web's Threads," *Arizona Republic,* July 19, 1995, pp. C1, C8.

Seltzer, Richard. "Heads Up," *Internet World,* April 1996, pp. 68–69.

Shimmin, Bradley. "Java to Leap Past Web," *LAN Times,* October 23, 1995, pp. 1, 26.

Sigler, Douglas. "HTML Toolbox," *Internet World,* April 1996, pp. 51–52.

Silverman, Robert. "On-line Transactions Are Safer Than You Think," *Communications Week,* November 6, 1995, pp. 1A, 12.

Snyder, Joel. "Good, Bad and Ugly Pages," *Internet World,* April 1996, pp. 26–27.

Sterne, Jim. "Missing the Point," *Network World,* September 1995, p. 25.

Venditto, Gus. "Dueling Tools," *Internet World,* April 1996, pp. 37–49.

Venditto, Gus. "Search Engine Showdown," *Internet World,* May 1996, pp. 79–86.

Welch, Douglas E. "Wanted: Good Cheap Web Space," *Network World,* November/December 1995, pp. 20–21.

Welz, Gary, "The Ad Game," *Internet World,* July 1996, pp. 50–57.

Wiggins, Richard W. "The Word Electric," *Internet World,* September 1995, pp. 30–33.

Wilder, Clinton, "Web Site Pays Off," *Information Week,* May 20, 1996, p. 41.

Doing Business on the World-Wide Web

Wresch, William. "New Lifelines," *Internet World,* November 1995, pp. 102–106.

Yahoo! Internet Life, "From Soup to Nuts: A One-Step Solution to Put Your Business On-line," May/June 1996, p. 14.

Yahoo! Internet Life. "Long Distance Service for the Price of Local," May/June 1996, p. XX.